15—

Corbit-Calloway Memorial Library
Odessa Delaware

THE HISTORY OF HYATTSTOWN

D1027911

THE HISTORY
OF
HYATTSTOWN

HERITAGE BOOKS, INC.

Copyright 1998

Dona Lou Cuttler

Published 1998 by

HERITAGE BOOKS, INC.
1540E Pointer Ridge Place
Bowie, Maryland 20716
1-800-398-7709
www.heritagebooks.com

ISBN 0-7884-0985-9

A Complete Catalog Listing Hundreds of Titles
On History, Genealogy, and Americana
Available Free Upon Request

ACKNOWLEDGEMENTS

Special thanks to Mike Dwyer, Historic Resources Manager at the Office of History and Archaeology, Montgomery County Park and Planning. Research on the town, and much of the background work was done by him. "Friends of Historic Hyattstown" compiled information on many of the houses, and supplied photographs, and additional information. Bob Price contributed the history of the Christian Church. Joann Woodson contributed the history of Montgomery Chapel and information on the black members of the community. Rev. Edwin Schell provided records for the Methodist Churches. Frank and Kitty Linthicum shared countless memories and information. Mary Wolfe Hertel and Margaret Myers did research and legwork when I was too far to find what was needed. The volunteers at the Montgomery County Historical Society and Jane Sween furthered my research and allowed the land patent overlay to be used. Mary Beth McDonough provided information and photographs. Elizabeth Miles Burdette kept me straight, house by house. Anice Lee Cecil Dancy kept me inspired. Louise Ehlers artisitc cover drawing represents the feel of Hyattstown and Ethel Wolfe Hebbard and kept me solvent through this process. Thank you all.

TABLE OF CONTENTS

Maps, Lists and Poems

PHOTO CREDITS

CHAPTER ONE

The land that became Hyattstown began as picturesque, rolling hills with a creek and natural resources. The earliest people to pass through the area could have been the Seneca and Piscataway Tribes. Part of the Seneca Trail followed the same path as the Georgetown Road would take in later years. The Piscataway Tribe re-located to the Potomac River west of Sugar Loaf Mountain, after leaving their lands in southern Prince George's County. As explorers pushed west from the original settlement of St. Mary's City, the vast acreage in upper Maryland was an enticement for land speculators.

During Colonial rule, persons who transported settlers from England could receive land grants from the crown. Also, wealthy Marylanders applied for land in newly opened areas as investments. Such was the case with Matthias Bordley. He had property surveyed for him containing 2,030 acres which he patented as "The Principal" in 1747. Adjacent to this property, but along the creek, 29 3/4 acres of a mill seat were patented as "Ivey Reach." At this time, all of this land was part of Prince George's County. When Samuel Cecil leased "The Principal" in 1751, Frederick County had been carved from Prince George's County. The lease was for 31 years with annual payments of 150 lbs. tobacco, in cask, shipped on the Potomac. In 1745 the road that connected the tobacco port of Georgetown to Frederick Town opened. It has been called by many names, The Georgetown Road, The Frederick Road, route 240, route 355 but, "The Great Road" is the best description for this town. It was supposed to be "two rails" or twenty-two feet wide, and maintained for travelers use. However, the Great Road was in horrible condition in April of 1755 when General Braddock and his troops moved from George-town to Frederick. Although his advance men cut through brush, Braddock's coach could not keep up the pace of the men on horseback. Road conditions caused considerable delays on his entire mission.

In 1748 Frederick County was created from Prince George's County. The county line dissected Matthias Bord-ley's land called "The Principal." Approximately 20 acres was now in Frederick County, at the top of the hill. The remainder stretched from west of the Great Road, as far as the modern I-270 interchange, to east of the road, near the current town boundaries.

Land Patents 1740's

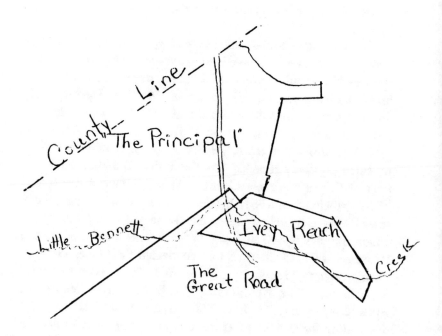

During the next 20 years the road was used by huckster, travelers and tobacco farmers rolling their product to market. Herds of animals were driven on the road and tolls were eventually set up to help offset the cost of maintenance in various sections. The more wear and tear you caused to the road surface, the higher the toll. Herds of cattle, teams of horses pulling a four wheel or more vehicle were charged higher rates than a single horse with a rider would pay.

In 1776 Montgomery County was created. Named for Richard Montgomery, it was one of the first acts to be passed by the newly independent politicians. At this time the area was part of Sugar Loaf Hundred where Zachariah Linthicum was the promoter of subscriptions for the War of Independence. He raised $1,333.00 in funds for the cause. Local blacksmith Nicholas Rhodes and two of his sons enlisted and were veterans of the Revolution, receiving pensions later in life. The Great Road became a military supply route during the wars years, as well as hosting troops in the local taverns. George Washington stopped at area taverns on his way to Frederick Town, and on return trips to Georgetown. During this era of stage coach travel, the taverns, or ordinaries, were located 15-20 miles apart. Stage coach drivers could count on making it that far in a day, when road conditions were good. Their passengers could get grog, supper and lodging for the night, and livery stables were available for the team of horses.

On March 2, 1779 the mill seat was advertised in the Maryland Journal and Baltimore Advertiser: "182 acres on Little Bennett Creek, send application to Jacob Harmon." Little Bennett Creek is a gentle, babbling water source that is not very powerful at the point where it crosses the Great Road. It is fordable, except during the spring thaw, and probably did not have a bridge over it at this time.

Matthias Bordley left his property, now in Montgomery and Frederick Counties to his son John and daughter-in-law Jane Bordley. In 1788 John sold 100 acres of "The Principal" to Edward Ward for 200 pounds. In 1791 Brice

3

Worthington and Thomas Beall sold "Ivey Reach" to Joshua Cecil.

As districts were laid out in the newly formed Montgomery County, Clark's tavern, also called Scholl's, was the polling place. The area became Clarksburg, and the district was named for the village. A mail stop was added for several places along the road, including one at the Little Bennett Creek. The tavern was located on the west side of the road, just north of the creek. It became a passenger stop on the stagecoach route in 1794. This area was flat and grassy, good for grazing and watering the teams, and convenient for the stagecoach drivers because of the two hills flanking the creek. At that time the road zigzagged back and forth up the hill, because the wagons and stagecoaches were unable to ascend straight up. The road bed was deeply rutted during the rainy season, and by tacking up the hill, horses had better footing.

After eyeing this natural stopping point, and the surrounding acreage, Jesse Hyatt purchased 207 acres of land from John Bordley for 415 pounds. This particular acreage was not suited to farming. The soil is rocky and when plowed, some farmers report a petroleum-like odor, and that the soil is "slick." Some of the water from local springs has a metallic taste. Slate is found in banks and cultivation was not the best use of the land.

So, as Federal Troops were being sent up the road to put down the Whiskey Rebellion in Pennsylvania, young Jesse Hyatt conceived the idea of creating a town, with quarter acres lots where people could establish businesses, and he could profit by selling the lots. He also devised an income plan, whereby he, and his heirs, would receive perpetual annual ground rent, after the purchase of the lot had been completed.

As the land was being surveyed, William Richards, the miller, passed away. George Wolfe became the next miller on Little Bennett Creek, where the tavern was in operation, with a distillery, mail was being delivered, stagecoaches passed twice a week, and Jesse Hyatt, now 33 years old, was planning

4

the town that bears his name. The 105 lots were laid out in double rows down each side of the Great Road, with alleys in between every fifth lot. He named the alley closest to the mill Gay Street, and the portion of the Great Road running through his town, Main Street.

Jesse Hyatt had the plan of the town recorded on March 9, 1798 in the Montgomery County Courthouse. Each boundary was marked by a stone bearing letters beginning with A. The lots had a front footage of 66 feet, and a depth of 165 feet. The subsequent alleys from south to north were named First, Second, and Third Alley. The lane paralleling the Great Road to the left was named East Lane, and to the right, West Lane. They were to be maintained at sixteen and a half feet wide. Main Street was to be three rails, or 66 feet wide.

The first lots to be sold were purchased by Henry F. Poole. He purchased lots 49 and 50 in 1798. The annual ground rent of five shillings was due each January 1, beginning in 1799. He built a cabin, and was the first storekeeper in the town, then known as Hyatt's Town.

Thomas Foster, the first blacksmith in the town, was conveniently located on the corner of Gay and Main Streets. After coming down either hill into town, the horses provided ample business. Jacob Smith purchased four lots the east side of Main Street and was the carpenter.

One of the first weddings in town was that of Mrs. Lavinia Hyatt Richards, widow of the late miller, William Richards, to George Wolfe. Mr. Wolfe purchased the mill, and farmed the land behind the miller's house. Lavinia's children from both marriages later founded the Christian Church of Hyattstown, and her grandson was a preacher there.

James Hinton was living in Eli and Belt Brashear's cabin in 1801, according to a advertisement in the <u>Georgetown Museum</u> on July 10. Richard Wooten's land sale was held at "James Hinton's dwelling house in Hyattstown." Other early landholders included, James Scott, who built a cabin next to Jacob Smith, Adam Ramshauer, Francis Puster, Charles

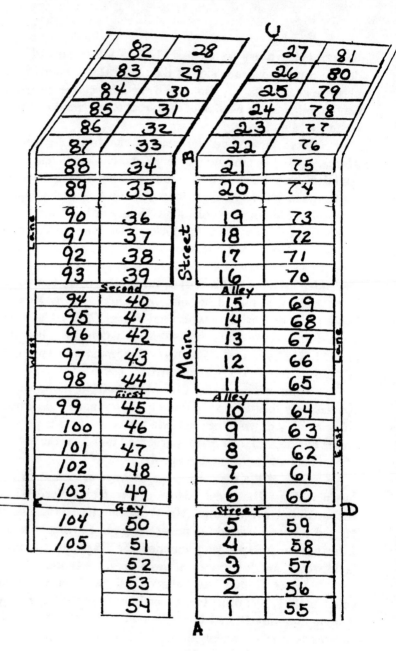

1798 Town Plat

6

Tabler, Joshua Inman, Barrick Hall, William Hyatt, Charles Busey, Jr., Lewis Duvall, Joshua Dorsey, William Burgess and Christian Tabler.

The Frederick-Town Herald lists the following items: Eli Hyatt claims a runaway horse at Hyatt's Town [June 25, 1803.] "Stop the Villain" George Davis warns about a horse thief in Hyattstown [June 16, 1804.] And the miller, George Wolfe, placed an advertisement for a runaway slave June 30, 1804.

By 1804 Jesse Hyatt owned 710 acres, ten slaves, and he was collecting ground rent from 12 owners. Hyatt's Town had six cabins, a tavern, and grist mill. Although a few crops were grown in the back of resident's dwellings, the life in the rural village centered around commerce. The road was maintained and services were provided to the travelers, because this was their primary industry. A petition was made for a road from Hyatt's Town to Liberty Town passing through New Market. This would eventually become route 75, but making sure that it went to Hyatt's Town was a strategic point for the merchants.

On March 6, 1804 Eli and Mary Ann Hyatt sold a half acre lot to the Trustee's of the Methodist Episcopal Church for a log building to be erected. One of the trustees, Charles McElfresh had been holding meetings for members. The other trustees were: John H. Smith, Joseph Benton, Samuel Hobbs and Basil Soper. Samuel Soper is credited with constructing the chinked log church, which set back farther from the road than the current building does. The outline of the original building is visible near the addition at the back of the church. Samuel Soper also taught classes on weekdays in this building. The school met here for about 25 years.

The Great Road at this time was a toll road, but not officially a turnpike. In 1805 local politicians pushed for the Georgetown to Frederick Road to be incorporated as a turnpike. On January 25, 1806 an act was introduced in the Assembly to attain turnpike status for the Great Road. This

7

would allow funding to be established for the maintenance of condition of the road.

In 1809 Hyatt's Town was officially incorporated, with town laws, by the State legislature. A resurvey was done by Hezekiah Neatch and recorded August 7, 1810 with very specific boundary marks, lots and streets. By the following year there were 12 residences in the village, including the new brick house being constructed for George Davis, and Levi Phillips ran advertisements for his tavern in local newspapers. Bishop Francis Asbury preached to a capacity crowd at the log church in 1811, before going on to New Market to preach.

The church did not have a stove in it at this time. During the winter, people brought tin boxes with them, containing hot coals to keep warm. Stoves were considered inappropriate for houses of worship and even in deep snows, services were well attended. Hymns were sung unaccompanied, and the circuit preacher had a four church circuit to serve. The Montgomery Circuit included Sugar Loaf Mountain Chapel, Clarksburg, Hyatt's Town and Lime Kiln.

The State Militia Acts of 1811 required all white males between 18-45 to serve, unless their religious beliefs exempted them, in which case they paid three dollars annually. Some occupations were also exempt: doctors, teachers, etc. Many of the Frederick County 2nd Regiment troops, which included Upper Montgomery County, marched through Hyattstown en route to Washington. Captain John Brengle's company marched from Frederick to Clarksburg August 25, 1814. Their orders were changed, and they returned to Clarksburg, before serving in Baltimore at the battle of North Point. John Hyatt was shot clean through in this battle, but recovered.

Nine companies of Frederick Militia were present at the Battle of Bladensburg including the First Cavalry District under the command of Major John Cook. The troops of horse of Captain Nicholas Hall were formed in Frederick of men from Monrovia and Hyattstown. Private Benjamin Beall

8

stated that he "volunteered at Hyattstown, " so the company may have ridden through on the Great Road. They served from August 7 until September 10, 1814. Following the defeat at Bladensburg, August 24, they saw action in the battle of Indian Head. They were discharged in Carroll County, and allowed five days for travelling home.

2nd Regiment, 1st Cavalry District

Nicholas Hall, Captain
Thomas Burgee, Jr., 1st Lieut.
Barrick Hall, 2nd Lieut.
Miel Burgee, Cornet

Daniel Collins, Qtr. M. Sgt.
Archibald Browning, 2nd Sgt.
John Montgomery, 3rd Sgt.
Henry Houser, 4th Sgt.

Privates:
Henry Baker, trumpeter
Benjamin Beall
Daniel Browning
William Carney
Benjamin Colehorse
George Davis
Isaac Davis
John Ellis
Elisha Fisher
John Griffith
Benjamin Hagan
Asa Hyatt
William Hyatt

Jacob Ijams
James Kinna
Edward Linton
William Lupton
Philip McElfresh, Jr.
John Miller
Samuel Paine
Joseph Purdy, Jr.
Joseph Purdy, Sr.
William Salmon
Philemon McElfresh Smith, Sr.
Paul Talbot
Ephraim Thornburgh
Asa Ward

The push for turnpike status was still in the fore front during the war, and the Turnpike Act was repeatedly revived at various times. The town continued to grow, and residents would soon reach the number needed to become a separate hundred. Jurisdictions were divided within Clarksburg District by population which counted taxables as white, male, landowners over 21 years of age. Once an area reached 100 taxables, they qualified for their own constable, and a tobacco inspector, as well as other needs. In 1813 town founder Jesse Hyatt died without a will. At the time he owned 1,206 acres contiguous to Hyatt's Town and six lots in town. His headstone is in the Christian Cemetery, south of the mill. He died just two years short of seeing the town that bears his name becoming a separate hundred.

The first constable, Daniel Collins, was a de-frocked priest from New York and a tailor by trade. As constable he was accused of taking bribes, and fined in Equity Court for accepting illegal fees. He left Hyattstown for the Great Falls area and a sale of his former property was held at Tabler's tavern in 1826.

For several years during this period camp meetings were held on Charles McElfresh's farm. Tent services were conducted and families came from Urbana, Thurston, Comus and surrounding areas. One such week is advertised in the Frederick Herald, July 8, 1815.

In 1817 the Washington Turnpike Company divided the Great Road into two sections to facilitate the construction of the road bed. From Tenallytown to Rockville was the first section and received priority funding. From Rockville to Williamsport was deemed section two. Federal funding was established for the National Road which was being constructed westward from Cumberland to the Ohio Valley. Once the Great Road was linked to the National Road, residents were convinced that Hyatt's Town would boom. In the village a storekeeper, blacksmith, carpenter-undertaker, physician, tailor, innkeeper, distiller and tavern keeper, church and gristmill

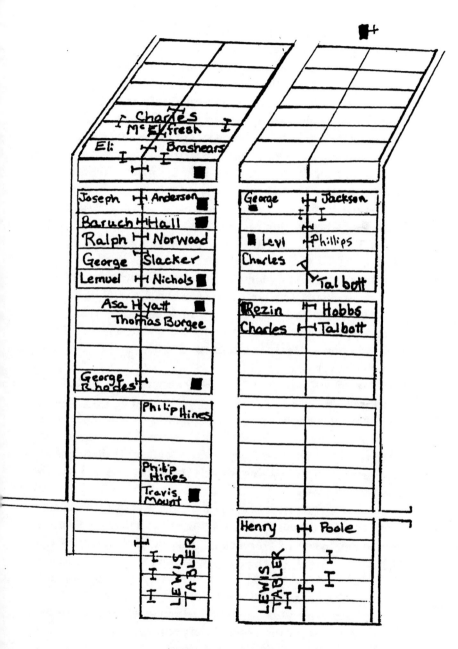

1820 TAX ASSESSMENT LIST

were all meeting the needs of the residents and travelers. But the road condition continued to be a serious issue. If it wasn't rutted from rain, it had ankle deep dust when a wagon went by.

The road was the source of news from other communities, and the Nation's Capitol. It brought the latest in fashion, imports and innovations by way of peddlers and travelers who stopped at the inn. The stage coaches of this era traveled about 12 miles per hour. Fare from Frederick to Georgetown was $3.00 and took from 3 AM to 7 PM. From Frederick to Baltimore was a 24 hour ride. Rates of toll: hogs, sheep cattle, 4 cents; horse with one rider, $2.00; two-wheel cart with horse $4.00; four wheel wagon with horse $8.00.

By 1822 stages left Frederick on Thursday and Friday mornings at 5 AM and arrived at 5 PM with a fare of $1.00 per passenger, with seating for 12. Some road improvements had been made by December of 1824 when General Lafayette passed Hyatt's Town on his way to Frederick. What was necessary was additional funding from a stable source. Montgomery County Banks subscribed $10,000 to be used for improvements to the Great Road.

In November of 1825 the 470 acre farm of the late Eli Hyatt was advertised in the Maryland Journal & True American. The following year, the same publication notes that there was a public sale at William Clark's tavern in September, and again in 1828. His two-story frame dwelling of three rooms above and three below was for sale in 1831, as he had moved closer to Rockville.

Merchants were also the dispenser's of medicine at this time. In 1829 Josiah Wolfe is listed as the agent for Hance's Compound Syrup of Horehound in an advertisement in the Maryland Journal & True American. One of the many elixirs of the day, customers could buy a bottle for just about anything that ailed them at the local mercantile.

This same year Andrew Jackson was en route to his presidential inauguration when he experienced the condition of the Great Road first hand. He stopped over night in Hyattstown and had the choice of staying at the Hyatt House, or the Tabler's Hotel. He is said to have chosen Tabler's because "That's where the wagoners stop." The residents and wagoners alike must have gotten their two cents worth in about the road's conditions at this chance town meeting. The road was vital to their local commerce, but they felt that it was now of national importance, as a link from the capitol city, to the West. The National Road stretched to St. Louis and yet the portion close only 30 miles from Washington was in miserable shape. After all, this would be their opportunity to express local concerns right to the top man himself. Educational facilities were also a concern of the residents at this time and Jackson heard many Americans voicing needs for schools.

President Jackson must not have remembered much about his journey down the Great Road, for he vetoed the turnpike bill, deeming it a local issue and not of national importance. However, the school did get built. The County bought one part of a back lot for the town to build a school in 1830. It was a pay school, where parents paid $2.50 per child, per semester to the teacher directly. The parents had the option of buying textbooks or renting them each semester. The teacher purchased the wood stove and rented it back to the parents.

The following year the Frederick Herald reported that a bill was before the House of Representatives to "Authorize an appropriation to turnpike the mail road between Rockville and Monocacy Bridge." There was also hope of paving the road at this time. Merchants in town continued to complain about the road's condition, as did their customers. Matthew Hannah advertised in the Maryland Free Press had a store in Hyattstown where he sold, cleaned, and repaired wheat fans and would exchange old ones for new. Wheat fans were used to clean and separate wheat before milling. He also made and sold household furniture, tables, chairs, bedsteads.

Newspapers would arrive in town on Wednesdays, brought on horseback from Frederick. As the stages came on

Thursdays and Fridays, this gave the travelers fresh news. Tavern fare was 62 and a half cents. This bought the visitor supper, lodging, morning and evening grog, plus gentlemen were offered cigars. Livery and whiskey were extra.

Residents of Hyattstown sought alternatives to farming, such as the mill, tavern, and stores. Lewis Tabler founded the tan yard on the creek that combined several functions. Zeigler's sumac mill, nearby, provided a source for the local hides to be soaked in. As local trees were cleared for timber, bark was used for tannin in large dipping vats at the tannery. Local saddle makers, shoe makers and bookbinders used the products, making the Hyattstown complex an industrial park.

On April 23, 1833 Indian Chief Blackhawk was escorted through town with his two sons. They were en route to Washington for hearings. Gay Street at the south end of town actually connected all the way to Barnesville. It was farm road, ungraded and had several streams to ford along the way. Since it led to Sugar Loaf Hundred, it was familiarly known as "Old Hundred" Road. In 1837 it was widened to 22 feet, and roots, rocks and stones were removed with picks and shovels. The section in front of each residents house was their responsibility to keep up. Fines were levied against those who let their segment go uncared for. The road supervisor for each area was appointed, and was unpaid for this thankless job. During this time period Eli Wolfe was the magistrate of Hyattstown and he built the brick mansion at the corner of Gay Street and West Lane. His son Jesse Hyatt Wolfe was born that year.

In March of 1834 Alexander Campbell came to the area on a preaching tour. The northeastern United States had been experiencing the "Great Awakening" and Campbell brought his message to the Upper Montgomery County people. A group of Hyattstown folks had been meeting as a congregation of "Disciples of Christ" and they appointed Trustees to build a church in 1837. The land for the church was donated by William E. Anderson. The 3/4 acre plot was originally part of "Wildcatt Springs" and by 1840 the log meeting house was

14

in use for their worship services.

In 1840 road construction on the Great Road improved the condition of the surface, but it had become evident to the population along the road that it would never attain turnpike status. Once the Baltimore and Ohio Railroad was going through Monrovia, Hyattstown could no longer hope for prominence. Coaches could now travel 18 miles a day, and Hyattstown was still a stop along the route. The road stretched 43 miles from Washington, and it still took 22 hours to go the entire distance. During this era, the Hyatt House was a nice place to stop. It had beautiful hard wood floors, and comfortable guest rooms. James K. Polk arrived in Hyattstown in 1845 en route to his inauguration and chose to stay at the Hyatt House over night.

Just four short years later wagons heading west in large numbers found the merchants of Hyattstown ready to supply their needs before leaving the civilized eastern section of the country. As the wagons headed for California and the idea of striking it rich hit local farmers, some of them decided to seek their fortunes and joined the Forty-Niners. One of these was Hammondatha Cecil. He left his wife, five children and farm chores behind to prospect for gold. Unfortunately, he died before he reached Sutter's Mill and the children were spilt up between three relatives. Such was the case with some of the pioneers, but others fulfilled their dreams.

For the local merchants the rush brought renewed business and excitement to the town. Medicine shows were popular at this time. Remedies for brain fatigue, fever, cholera, toothaches, and earaches were sold from wagons that passed through town. Physicians were trained by apprenticing with an area doctor for an agreed period of time. Druggists often mixed their own ingredients in the store. Tincture of ginger was concocted by dripping water through ginger root, and catching it below in bottles. Medicine was dispensed in paper trifolds. If you were sent to the store for cough drops, you could select 10 and put them in a paper to

15

take home. For medicines that had to be taken at specific intervals, a small time counter that burned oil could be read to see how many hours had passed since the last dosage. Not many of the medicines actually alleviated symptoms, or cured cases.

The Methodist Episcopal Church burned to the ground in 1852. They may have met in the school for a time, because the cornerstone for a the current building was not laid until 1856. The new structure was begun in June of that year by local contractor, John Gardner, following the ceremony conducted by Rev. Charles Reed. The two-story brick building was in the Greek Revival style and had a gallery upstairs for the slaves to attend services. The dedicatory sermon was preached by Rev. Benjamin F. Brown. By this time the Montgomery Circuit included Sugar Loaf Chapel, Hyattstown, Bennett Creek Chapel and Clarksburg.

However, a growing number of Methodists were divided over the issue of slavery. Bishop Asbury had preached against the owning of other humans, but some Methodists hesitated to free the slaves that they had purchased. This difference resulted in a denominational schism. The Methodist Protestant Church broke away from the Methodist Episcopal Church, forming the "Southern" Methodists. Members began meeting separately with Rev. John P. Hall in 1865, and eventually built another building.

For entertainment the Hyattstown Brass Band was formed, and featured in a Montgomery Sentinel advertisement: "Honor to whom honor is due: The Hyattstown Brass Band, being composed of young men, principally mechanics, who have been at an expense of nearly $1,000 each having equal interest in that it's own expense for the benefit of our country are now competent to fulfill any engagement that might be called for with the latest choice of music such as quick steps, polkas, waltzes, gallops, reels, funeral marches. We trust that the citizens when they have a call for music will as honor due, give us a favorable consideration. Our motto is: Not to be

excelled by any band in the county.
U. M. Layton, leader
C. T. Anderson, director.
J. C. D. Harris, sec'y.
J. H. Tabler treasurer.

Ethel Cecil

CHAPTER TWO

Four months after Ft. Sumter was fired upon in the Charleston harbor, Union Regulars of General Nathaniel Banks were camped at the Little Bennett Creek. The scenic spot that had been a drawing card to the area in the first place, also made a natural spot for troops to set up their tents. The encampment was temporary, and the soldiers moved on to Darnestown, where they set up communications and observation areas.

On August 19, 1861 Company F of the 12th Massachusetts Volunteers camped at Little Bennett Creek in Hyattstown on their way to Clarksburg. They were under the command of Captain Kimtall. He had intelligence reports mentioning munitions and arms stored at the Davis House, then occupied by Nicholas Worthington. A detail of 20 men accompanied Captain Kimtall to the Worthington House to search for materials. The only arms they found were a few old muskets of the Revolutionary War era.

On August 26 Union troops were still in the vicinity, scouting from the hills around Hyattstown and 10,000 troops were reviewed. Signal corps set up atop Sugar Loaf Mountain. Throughout the war this was a strategic spot to control. War correspondent "Porte Crayon" sketched the army encampment at Hyattstown for Frank Leslie's Illustrated Newspaper.

In December the army began moving to it's winter headquarters in Frederick, traveling up the Great Road. Most of the winter months during the war years, the men drilled and did not interfere with civilians. Many residents got on with the routine of their everyday lives, except for the tavern keepers, who saw good business from couriers and officers.

In September 1862, General Wade Hampton's Brigade of J. E. B. Stuart's Confederate Cavalry set up outposts in Hyattstown before the Antietam Campaign, as part of the cavalry screen stretching from Poolesville to New Market.

Ascending Long Hill, Hyattstown, Maryland

Topographical Headquarters, Hyattstown, Maryland

During a skirmish on the ninth, three pickets were killed and one man was wounded by Lt. Easton and four of his men on the road leading out of Hyattstown. This sent the company of reserves scurrying back to the foot of the hill leading to town. Later that evening Stuart's men were attending a party in Urbana when the First Union Cavalry under the command of Captain Reno began to advance. The men left the dance floor to challenge the unit and fired on them as they entered Hyattstown. During the skirmish, Hyattstown resident Mary Jane Beall took her infant son Robert Edgar to the basement of their home for safety. After the Federal's retreated, Stuart and his troops returned to the dance floor. Near Sugar Loaf Mountain, three officers were taken prisoner by Union troops. Confederates returned to Nicholas Worthington's house, this time demanding food. They took 90 bushels of corn, 30 bushels of oats, and hay. Worthington later requested reimbursement, which he did not receive.

On September 11 and 12 Union General Sumner's 2d Corps Army of the Potomac passed through Hyattstown, on their way to South Mountain and Antietam. They held the road and signal station on Sugar Loaf for several days.

In August 1863 the Union 6th Corp was stationed at Hyattstown en route to the battle of Gettysburg. Their stay was brief and the mood was somber.

In October 1863 J. E. B. Stuart was sent on a raid to Chambersburg, Pennsylvania with 1,800 men. He was asked to destroy the railroad bridge, bring back fresh horses and supplies without taking any from civilians. The troops left Virginia and traveled to Chambersburg via Hagerstown. During the raid Captain Blackford found a detailed map of Franklin County, allowing Stuart to chose alternate routes for retreat. The men took Federal supplies, horses, weapons and food, but failed to destroy the iron railroad bridge. Due to the intense rain, the Potomac River was too deep to cross where they had previously forded, and Federal troops were placed all along the river. So Stuart turned his men toward Emmitsburg, where his men were given bread, meat, and buttermilk and kept moving to avoid the Union soldiers behind them. Stuart then split his forces, one column headed for Mouth of Monocacy and the other for Monrovia. General George Stoneman and the 8th Cavalry Regulars were near Dickerson waiting with strong artillery. Alfred Pleasanton and 800 Cavalry were near Mechanicstown with troop trains waiting to attack Stuart's men as soon as they could be cornered. The main column proceeded to Hyattstown under a blanket of fog, eluding the sentinels atop Sugar Loaf Mountain. The men had marched 55 miles, but the next 12 were the most dangerous. All four fords were being guarded by Federal troops. As the fog lifted, the troop's movements were spotted by the signal corp and reported to be heading for Dickerson. But Stuart had a local man in his ranks. Captain White knew the back roads, and led the men up Old Hundred Road to Monocacy Church where Stuart learned that Stoneman and his men were in Poolesville. Just one and a half miles from the Monocacy they encountered Pleasanton and his men. The two forces skirmished, but Pleasanton was pushed aside, leaving Stuart an opening at White's Ford.

Col. E. R. Biles and three companies of the 99th Pennsylvania Infantry were deployed along the rim of the rock quarry nearby. Lee, who was leading the other column, spotted the 99th, halted and consulted with his officers. He threatened an all out attack if Biles did not surrender. As the signal corp had spotted Stuart, Biles knew reinforcements could arrive for Lee. Biles took his time debating his next step. After 15 minutes Lee signaled to Pelham, who began firing cannon. The 99th withdrew, the guns moved across the Potomac River into position to cover the crossing, and the column crossed safely.

Stuart's men covered 80 miles in 24 hours. In his daring raid he brought back reconnaissance, $250,000 in Federal supplies, and hundreds of horses at a cost of one man wounded and two missing. J. E. B. Stuart and his troops celebrated their safe return to Virginia for several days.

In December, 1863 Charles Frederick Linthicum came home on a furlough. He spent Christmas with his family on the farm one mile from Hyattstown and told them about his experiences at the battle of Gettysburg. Captain Linthicum had escaped with a slight wound from a minie ball, but had had two horses shot out from under him, and was the only survivor of his unit. This would be his last visit, as he was killed at the battle of Cold Harbor six months later. Following his visit, his father John Hamilton Smith Linthicum was arrested and taken prisoner to the Old Capitol in Washington. He never knew what his crime was, or who had accused him but was held until the end of the war. After his release, he returned to farming at the foot of Sugar Loaf Mountain.

Captain Charles Frederick Linthicum

The battle of Monocacy was fought north of Urbana, on the Great Road July 9, 1864. The covered bridge was destroyed and reportedly, the river ran red following the battle from casualties and wounded. General Early's troops passed through Hyattstown swiftly, on their way to Washington on July 10, hoping to take the capitol. Although they won the battle, the delay at Monocacy had allowed additional Union troops to be deployed, successfully defending the District of Columbia.

On July 27, Early's men returned to their Virginia headquarters, while the 6th and 9th corp Army of the Potomac were in Hyattstown, planning to go to Harper's Ferry. As the 2d Continental Heavy Artillery 6th corp moved along the Great Road Louis Bissell noted the condition of the towns he passed. On August 1 he wrote: "On the road up from Washington we passed through the village of Rockville. It's a dirty place to my eye. The village next to Rockville is Hyattstown. This place has a much neater appearance."

The assassination of President Lincoln on April 14, 1865 occurred on Good Friday. During the Easter weekend celebration, several of the Hyattstown boys got rowdy and boisterous, as was the custom of this period. Perhaps it was ill-timed, as the country was mourning the president's death. Seven of the boys, including Warner Wellington Welsh and William Wallace Welsh, were charged with disloyalty and placed under military arrest. They were taken to Fort Dix, near Baltimore, where they were held and treated as prisoners. In the War Department, Union friends were able to use their influence to convince authorities that the boys were not part of any conspiracy plot or linked to the death of the president in any way. Six weeks later, they were finally released.

CHAPTER THREE

In the years following the war the population of Hyattstown continued to grow. The town now included 150 residents, two blacksmiths, two schoolhouses, a postmaster, four churches, three carpenters, an undertaker, physician, miller, shoemaker, carriage maker, churn maker, saddle and harness maker, cooper, and the tan yard. The slate quarry was in operation, as William Williams, slate roofer of Hyattstown, advertised his business in the <u>Montgomery Sentinel</u> of August 4, 1871.

The new Christian Church building was dedicated in 1871. The congregation had outgrown the old church and the new sanctuary was built in the middle of town. About 40 members were active when the present church opened it's doors to the community.

In 1875 the cornerstone was laid for the Methodist Protestant Church in Hyattstown, across from the Methodist Episcopal Church. William A. Wade was the pastor at this time and the circuit was ironically called the Montgomery Circuit, the same as the Methodist Episcopal Church. There were 20 members attending when the church was dedicated in 1876.

That same year the Hyattstown Singer Sewing Machine office opened. Isaac M. Singer introduced the "live payment plan" making this modern convenience affordable in installments. Levi Zeigler, the Singer agent, built a small shop next to his house where machines could be demonstrated, or taken in wagons to rural areas.

The schoolhouse was now 46 years old, and inadequate for the growing town. The community requested a new building in 1876, but the school board denied the request, as some areas did not even have a school building at the time. On the third annual try, a new school was promised. "Swamp College" closed in 1880 when the new two-room schoolhouse was completed.

Winters of this time period were more severe than recent seasons have been. There was more snow and a longer span of cold temperatures, which killed off more insects and produced higher spring freshets. Crops did not need pesticides to combat the infestations of destructive bugs, because their larvae were killed off during the winters. In the spring of 1881 "The Great Flood" covered the bridge over the Little Bennett Creek, and damaged the mill. The road washed out even worse than it usually did.

In 1884 George Butler, a black landowner, donated land along the Great Road for a church. The Montgomery Chapel was moved from the site of the former Christian Church up Long Hill on logs. The church's first pastor, William P. Ryder, came in 1886.

Gold fever struck again, this time closer to home. In June of 1892 the Baltimore Sun reported that gold was found on the Thomas Price farm near Hyattstown. The BH Gold Mine was established by local capitalists and later a Philadelphia Company leased the land. Smaller quantities of gold were found on other local farms.

An economic downturn swept the nation in the 1890's. Jacob S. Coxy conceived the plan for government relief and planned the first million man march on Washington, D. C. The plan was front-page news in every paper in the country, and as the march progressed through Maryland toward the Capitol, people in Hyattstown and Rockville kept an eye out for the "Army of the Commonweal of Christ." Coxy's right-hand man, Marshall Browne, held the belief that all souls were formed with a few of Christ's molecules in them, but that he and Coxy had an disproportionate supply.

Before setting out on the march, Coxy had promoted his scheme by having the "Good Roads Bill" introduced in Congress by Senator William Peffer. Peffer later introduced Coxy's "Non-Interest bearing-bond bill" with minimum wages for the unemployed to fix up the nations roads. While it sounded good, Coxy did not have any concept of the fear and terror his marchers would arouse in middle-class communities that they passed through.

They arrived in Frederick, where one man was arrested for pulling a knife on another man. They planned to stop on Little Bennett Creek the following night, and at this time Montgomery County had prohibition, so the residents were looking forward to a relatively peaceful, law abiding group. Each night's encampment was named in honor of some one significant, and the Little Bennett camp was named "Henrietta" for Coxy's wife. With him was his daughter Mamie, second wife Henrietta, and son "Legal Tender" Coxy, Marshall Browne, "Cyclone" Kirland, Honore Jaxson, Douglas Kallum, "Oklahoma Sam" and 286 other assorted men. The banner they carried read "Peace on Earth good will to men, He hath risen but death to interest on bonds."

"Cyclone" Kirland was an astrologer and con-man from Pittsburgh. Honore Jaxson, a half breed Indian, wore leather breeches, a white sombrero and a blanket. Douglas Kallum brought along copies of his book to sell on the way. It was entitled "Dogs and Fleas by one of the Dogs."

Marshall Browne dressed in the style of Buffalo Bill. He had the buckskin coat with Mexican half dollars for buttons. His gray beard was streaked with white and his hair was unkept. Coxy was a smaller man with glasses and not as flamboyant as Browne.

On Thursday afternoon the 26th of April, 1894 the men came marching down the Great Road, and in to Hyattstown. Knowing they were coming, the entire town was out to greet the crowd. Some offered food, housing, or stables. Others were curious about the men, and what Coxy had to say. Jacob Coxy backed up against a telegraph pole on Main Street in the middle of town and made an impromptu speech. The farmers and residents listened to his philosophy and then the army walked to the creek.

The welcome the men received at Hyattstown was said

27

to have exceeded every other stop on the march, which began in Ohio. "Camp Henrietta" stretched from the meadow of the Murphy farm all the way to the mill. At that time a suspension bridge crossed the Little Bennett Creek and the only men in the group that were able to cross it with out falling off were the ones who had served as sailors, for they could walk in unison. At suppertime tin plates were passed to the men. At 8 o'clock PM the camp was opened to visitors, with an admission price of a dime. The canvas tent was the site of the service which included the trick horses, speeches, and the doctrines of the group. Women and children could get in free with a paying gentleman. The Murphy family must have repeated the story of this event frequently. Their daughter Anice was only a year old when Coxy's army camped there, but she related stories associated with the event all of her life.

That night several con-men were running a shell game. Perry Watkins was the victim, until two detectives from the Metropolitan Police force, Horne and Byrd, removed the men from the tents. The men then played cards among themselves, and then set out for Gaithersburg in a stolen wagon. The farmer went after them in a buggy, and caught up with them.

Coxy's men slept on straw, in tents, then moved on to Rockville the next day. They eventually reached Brightwood Park, NW Washington, D. C. Coxy did contribute two lasting reform alternatives: Staging media events and marching on Washington.

The year after Hyattstown's Centennial a blizzard in February. The snow was so deep that even the hitching posts could not be seen. It was about this time that the poem about Hyattstown was written by Mr. Mullikin. One can notice that even the town doctor was sick.

In 1900 there were 275 residents in Hyattstown. Two schools are listed with 22 enrolled in the two-room school and five listed at the colored school. At this time there were two merchants, each with a salesclerk, two dressmakers, two millers, two plasterers, a Justice of the Peace, two wheat threshing machine operators, an undertaker, carpenter, physician, rural mail carrier, blacksmith, house painter, a laundress, mid-wife, a post rail maker and the creamery had opened.

In 1903 the Hyattstown Slate Quarry was outfitted with new machinery and by 1904 was back in operation. E. Brook Lee made a speech in Hyattstown on a carriage block c. 1918 to the concerned citizens regarding the condition of the Great Road. He convinced the citizens to surrender the town's incorporation in exchange for having the road paved. Progress was slow and anxiously anticipated. The road bed was altered. The bridge over Little Bennett Creek had to be constructed. On Long Hill, the road was changed to the west side of the cemetery. Previously one would have entered from east of the Christian Church Cemetery.

Listed in the 1920 census: Three merchants, two ministers, a stock dealer, blacksmith, huckster, post master and assistant post mistress, an auctioneer, four carpenters, two millers, a wheel wright, rural mail carrier, saw mill operator, laundress, auto machine machinist, creamery and 18 students in the school. Not listed were some of the mid-wives in Hyattstown: Emily Smith, Mary Rivers Hill, Mida Hawkins Jenkins Gray, and Georgia Randolph Snowden. Oliver Gray, blacksmith, John Price, shoemaker and Elias Price harness and saddlemaker—also barbered for the black residents of the village. Albert Jenkins is pictured in front of the tailor shop. He did odd jobs for anyone who needed a handy man.

The following year stone for the bridge over the Little Bennett Creek was hauled in. The road at this time was called 240, Old Georgetown Road. During the re-routing of the road, electricity came to Hyattstown. The road paving was done by the M. J. Grove Lime Co. who's trucks were very busy hauling concrete during this time. On June 16 one of the trucks hit and killed Charles Murphy, the miller, as he walked home. The final batch of concrete was poured on September 3, 1925. On September 25 a celebration was held at Mountain View Park. 55 men from the Grove Co. and officials from the contracting firm were the guests of the citizens of Hyattstown at a delightful dinner.

The paving of the road brought an unexpected turn of events. Merchants had long hoped the road improvements would bring additional business to the town. By the time the road was paved, people were able to travel in to Frederick for shopping excursions. But the road was still the scene of parades, Presidential motorcades en route to Camp David, and ever increasing traffic.

When telephone service came to Hyattstown party lines offered everyone's conversations as a source of gossip. Each house had a distinct ring pattern. However, there was nothing to stop someone else from picking up and listening in, except for integrity. But as is the case with modern conveniences, private service was eventually available.

Until recent years there was no bank in Hyattstown. Many people kept cash in their house and felt safe in the neighborhood. The exception to this may have been in June of 1927. Mr. Dorsey McElfresh was supervising road repairs near his home, just out side of town. William Henry Ross was repairing roads nearby for Mr. McElfresh, and noticed Mrs. Lottie McElfresh in the yard hanging laundry. He attacked and killed her, when she resisted him. Men from Hyattstown assisted in the search for Ross, and he was eventually convicted and hanged for the crime.

Elizabeth Miles Burdette was picking blackberries nearby and remembers hearing the screams. Not knowing until later what the cause was, the event left a deep impression with her. The brutal nature of the crime shook the community and stayed in the news for a long time.

Burdette Brothers Chevrolet dealership opened for business that year. Located next to Dudrow's Store, Burdette Brother's is a landmark in the area.

Gypsies camped in the woods behind the school house. They wore scarves and scared the local children that walked to school. This was beyond the remains of the Layton home called "The Orchard." They were seasonal visitors, chased out by the local men.

When the Depression hit, local families helped one another through hard times. People in Hyattstown have always looked out for their elderly neighbors and brought them dinner, vegetables from the garden. The churches have active members and the hometown spirit is alive and well.

Clifton Darby and Ethel Cecil

PHYSICIANS PRACTICING IN HYATTSTOWN:

B. J. Hershey   1850's
N. Joshua Hatcher b 1810 in Virginia moved to Hyattstown
from Poolesville to practice medicine.
Asa Hamilton Zeigler 1839-1882
Alexander L. Ransone 1847-1899, born in Norfolk, Va
and served as a cavalryman in the Confederate Army.
After the war, he practiced medicine in Baltimore for
several years, then Mt. Airy. He later moved to Hyattstown.
In 1900 Curtin M. Englar is listed in the census as the physician.
He was born in Maryland in July of 1873 and boarded with the
Bowman family.
Clifton Dronenburg is listed as a surgeon in the 1920 census.

Carroll Harn —one of Stuarts men

Postmasters of Hyattstown

Eli Wolfe	3 Jan 1832
Philemon M. Smith	30 May 1837
Joseph Anderson	30 May 1837
Josiah Wolfe	18 Dec 1841
James Birnside	18 Dec 1841
Levi T. Hyatt	30 Apr 1844
Asa Hyatt	19 Apr 1847
Josiah Wolfe	27 Mar 1848
Philemon M. Smith	11 May 1849
Jacob Umstead, Jr.	2 Nov 1853
John H. Wolfe	25 Jul 1854
David A. Zeigler	23 Apr 1856
Levi T. Hyatt	29 Mar 1858
Zachariah Brown	13 Sep 1860
Ezra Tabler	23 Apr 1860
William Richards, Jr.	3 Sep 1861
Joseph R. Smith	12 Nov 1861
Warner W. Welsh	13 Aug 1885
Levi C. Zeigler	16 Apr 1890
Richard H. Bowman	3 May 1894
Bradley H. Dudrow	21 Jun 1898

Rural delivery: horse-drawn wagon
carriers included: Mr. Purdum,
Irby Thompson and Clarence Day

PATRONS OF HYATTSTOWN POST OFFICE 1882

Businesses

Benton, S. M. and brothers, General Merchants
Brengle, John H., painter
Burdette, J. E., harnessmaker
Darby, George A., miller
Dudrow, Philip C., carpenter
Dutrow, Jacob W., blacksmith
Dutrow, Otho William, blacksmith
Gardner, John D., Justice of the Peace
Gardner, Edward Grafton and brothers, undertakers
Grimes, William L., shoemaker
Price, Levi, distiller
Smith, Joseph R., carpenter and Post Master
Tabler, Andrew Jackson, restaurant
Welsh, Wellington Warner, General Merchant
Zeigler, Asa Hyatt, physician
Zeigler, Levi Christopher, sewing machine agent

RESIDENTS

Anderson, Ellen
Benton, T. S.
Browning, Charles T.
Cecil, George Mortimer
Cecil, Otho Franklin
Cecil, Wilson Hammond
Grimes, John E.
Harris, Z. Gaither
Hawkins, Benjamin
Holland, James
Holland, Nathan
Johnson, Benjamin
Johnson, Levin B.
Keith, Caleb
Lawson, James U.
Leather, Edward
Lewis, William B.
Lewis, William F.
Linthicum, Cassidy
McLean, James
Miles, Lemuel
Murphy, Horace

Ordeman, F.
Price, Charles
Price, George F.
Price, Thomas of E.
Price, Thomas H.
Simmons, Abraham R.
Simmons, Samuel T.
Soper, John N.
Tabler, Andrew J.
Tabler, George F.
Tabler, John H.
Tabler, William
Warfield, Garrison
Warfield, Hamilton
Watkins, Luther
Watkins, W. T.
Welsh, Asa Hyatt
Whipp, Warren
White, James
Williams, William
Windsor, John
Wolfe, Jesse Hyatt

HYATTSTOWN

by Richard O. Mullikin
1892

You're attention I ask for a minute or two
While I in a few words, will tell you
Of a little village, nay rather a town,
Which I recognize as Hyattstown.

How old it is I cannot find out,
But you will say without any doubt,
That this little town has stood the blast
For many and many a winter past.

The people here are as good and kind
As any one would wish to find.
And if no one objects, I'll name a few
And tell you what some of them do.

I'll begin on the right, at the head of the town
And name each house until I get down
to the creek. Over the road I'll go
and then return on the other side, slow,

The church What a better place could I wish
To stand at the head of my long list?
'Tis here the people once a week as a rule
Assemble for preaching or Sunday School.

Many a warning from time to time
Is heard from the lips of the grand "Divine"
Bro. Will Hammond, who boards right near
With the pleasant family of Mrs. Gardner.

In the family are mother and children two
Elsie and Eddie and a Miss Grimes too,
And besides boarding a Methodist preacher,
They were so kind as to take a school teacher.

From this quiet home I go below
To a house where lives a Mr. Dudrow.
Mr. and Mrs. have children none,
But I must pass on down the line,

To Dr. Ransone's house of brick
Who, though a Dr., has been quite sick;
He was a victim of "La Grippe"
Out of whose clutches not many slip.

One step and now we come
To house tow families live in one,
A Mrs. Brengle, and along with her
A Mr. and Mrs. Koehler

Mr. Brengle is a painter by trade,
Just look at his home and you'll see he has made
Quite a change with his brush,
But I must hurry on with a rush.

Leaving this quiet, peaceful home
To that of Mr. Tabler we'll come
And below him a man living a happy life.
With no one to bother him but his wife.

A little further just back from the road,
We come to another house of God,
'Tis here the people meet once a week,
The straight and narrow way to seek.

To the left of the church just over the road
We come to house—the children's abode
And hastening on, the next on my list,
Is a house where lives a Mr. Lewis.

And now only one step more
And we come to a house known as the store,
I cannot name the things on the shelves,
You had better go and look for yourselves.

And hurrying on a little faster,
I come to the house of the Postmaster,
He and his wife and children three
Are just as happy as they can be.

And down the hill to the right is set
The house of Mr. Webb Burdette,
A little further on the verge
You will see the house of Mrs. Dronenburg.

And now farmers take care of your lambs
For on the hill the Wolfe mansion stands
And just below all in view,
Stands Mr. Burdette's and Thompson's too.

Over the road is Darby's mill,
The people here their sacks do fill
With flour and meal and buckwheat too.
Were it not for the miller, what would we do?

The next house I name on my way
Is where lives the barber, Cronen Gray.
And next with everything is style
Is the store and house of Mr. Pyles.

And now we'll skip a good big space:
The next in line is a pretty place,
Owned by Mr. Johnson and further on
Stands the house of Mr. Anderson.

And now my hearers what would we do
Were it not for Chas. Stewart to mend our shoes?
Mr. Rhodes comes next who "by the way"
Teaches a school just over the way.

Mr. Bowman the merchant, comes next in line,
And on a little further we'll find
The house of Mr. Peters, standing still.
Mr. Peters himself, works at the mill.

Going a little further we'll come first come
To a neat little house, Mr. Gardner's home.
And beyond this the blacksmith shop
Where Mr. Will Dudrow works with his "Pop."

And now only a step or so
Brings us again to a Mr. Dudrow
And beyond his home near the road
We will find another house of God.

My friends, I am come to the end of the line,
Look if you wish don't find
Things are just the way I stated to you,and if you
Why then I'm mistaken and much so too.

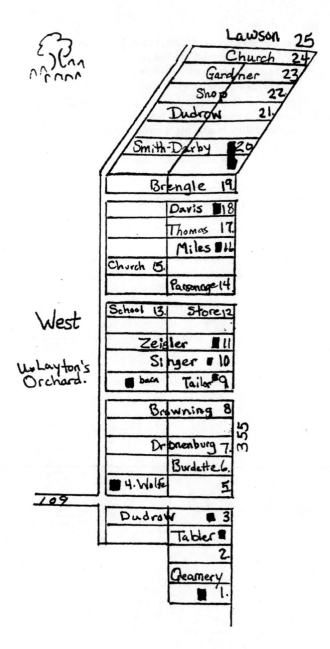

Lawson 25
Church 24
Gardner 23
Shop 22
Dudrow 21.
Smith-Darby 20

Brengle 19.

Davis 18
Thomas 17.
Miles 16
Church 15.
Parsonage 14
School 13. Store 12
Zeidler 11
Singer 10
barn Tailor 9
Browning 8
Dr. Onenburg 7.
Burdette 6.
4. Wolfe 5

Dudrow 3
Tabler
2
Creamery
1.

West

Wm Layton's
Orchard.

109

355

West Side—Great Road

40

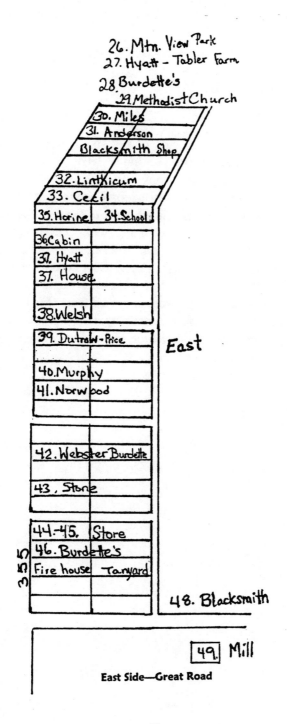

26. Mtn. View Park
27. Hyatt - Tabler Farm
28. Burdette's
29. Methodist Church
30. Miles
31. Anderson
Blacksmith Shop
32. Linthicum
33. Cecil
35. Horine | 34. School
36. Cabin
37. Hyatt
37. House
38. Welsh
39. Dutraw - Price
East
40. Murphy
41. Norwood
42. Webster Burdette
43. Stone
44.-45. Store
46. Burdette's
Fire house | Tanyard
48. Blacksmith
49. Mill

East Side—Great Road

41

ALONG THE GREAT ROAD

1. Price's Creamery
lots 53 & 54

South of 109 on the west side of the street, across from the present fire house, site of the block barn. The creamery opened in 1892 and was owned and operated by Willie W. Price. The operation centered around separating the cream from whole milk. Farmers milked early in the morning and set the five gallon jugs out on the main road. The horse-drawn milk wagon collected the jugs and took them to the creamery, leaving empty jugs for the next day at each farm. A few farms separated their own cream, but most sent theirs to the local creamery. After the cream was separated from the whole milk, it was taken to Monrovia and sent by railroad cars to Baltimore. The creamery operated for about 45 years. Raymond Price later ran a dairy farm here.

2. Site of the Tabler-Price Hotel:
lots 51-52

Lewis Tabler moved to Hyattstown from Jefferson in 1805. He purchased 15 acres with a tavern house. He ran the tavern and operated a distillery, manufacturing whiskey. He also kept a store at this location. In 1827 he advertised the tavern for sale: "Lewis Tabler's Tavern, log house of Elisha, is for sale with lots in town." In 1829 General Jackson was en route to his Presidential inauguration and stopped here for the night. By 1831 Andrew Jackson Tabler, son of Lewis, was running the establishment and bred horses here. Later, his son William was the tavern keeper and tanner of Hyattstown, along with another son, Abraham who was a tanner and miller in Hyattstown. The hotel was later operated by the Will W. Price family, but the structure is no longer standing. Presently a brick rambler stands on this site.

hotel, hyattstown, Md., W. W. Price, Prop.

3. Dudrow House
lots 50 & 104

This two-story frame house with wide verandah has been remodeled several times. Built by Webster Burdette for his parents c. 1910, Bradley Hill Dudrow later acquired it for his residence. Mr. Dudrow owned the first automobile in town. His daughter Dorothy Dudrow lived there before Fred Smith owned it.

4. Wolfe--Manion House
lots 102 & 103

Home of Jesse Wolfe, Justice of the Peace, later of Vernon Manion. An elegant brick house built in the 1840's with four corner chimneys, beautiful interior features, and a dumb waiter. It was by far the largest house in Hyattstown. Because of the sunken kitchen, part of the house was three stories high, with the bedrooms on the third floor. The house sat 250 feet back from 355, off 109 up on the hill. After the Manions moved the house was vacant until 1951 when it was torn down to make room for the present house.

5. Site of Foster's Blacksmith Shop
lot 49

Thomas Foster, the first blacksmith in Hyattstown, ran a smithy on this corner. In 1820, it was owned by Thomas Mount. This was an ideal location for his smithy to serve traffic from both roads. Jacob W. Dutrow operated the smithy from 1870-1900. This lot later was the site of Burdette's Funeral Home, where bodies were embalmed, and where he kept his horse-drawn hearse. Funerals at this time were held in the parlor of people's homes, directed by Webster Burdette. For four years, the upstairs of this structure was used as an upper grades school. Louise Miles Thompson, Silas Beall, Dorothy Dudrow, Richie Benson, Mary Ryan, Nell and Luther Thompson attended eighth and ninth grade classes. The hall was later used for church suppers and a pool table was available for the men.

6. Burdette House
lot 48

Owned by Philip Hines in 1820, William W. Dutrow later had a large house on this lot. In 1915 Edward Dolston Burdette replaced the previous house with the bungalow style presently on this site.

7. Dronenburg House
lot 47

This lot was sold at the 1870 Tabler Trustee sale and at that time had no buildings on it. The house was originally built for Thomas Dronenberg in 1876 and Cornelia is shown living there in 1879. Horace Dronenberg was the last one to live here before the house was torn down. Lot 46 had a well on it in 1870, but no house.

8. Perry Browning House
lot 45 south of First Alley

Owned by Philip Hines in 1820, this lot was later owned by Abraham Tabler and then, in 1870, by John H. Tabler. At that time it had "a fine frame stable, 20 X 30 feet divided into convenient stalls and covered with slate" from the Hyattstown Quarry. It was next purchased by Perry T. Browning for $183.50. In 1876 Perry had a 2 1/2 story frame house built close to the road with two interior end chimneys and a red standing seam tin roof. The front porch had four Victorian bracketed columns. Perry died there in 1880. Son Charles T. lived there until 1907, then John and Elizabeth Beall rented the house in 1913 and later purchased it. After John's death in 1917, Elizabeth married Ernest F. Harris. The house was sold in 1961.

Alleys

Up First Alley, heading west was "The Orchard" home of Uriah Layton. It was located on West Lane and the alley was beautifully lined with apple trees. This house is no longer standing, but the lane still exists. The tailor shop is visible in the lower left of the photograph.

9. Tailor Shop
lots 44 & 98

George Rhoades owned these lots in 1820. The frame building for the tailor shop was built by John Gardner in 1860. In 1869, Layton sold the property at a constable's sale to John M. Zeigler, the highest bidder. The property changed hands from Abraham Tabler, to James H. Williams for $375 in 1870, to Caroline S. Leather in 1872. Davis rented the tailor shop from the Leather family. Webster V. Burdette bought it in 1890 from the heirs of Caroline Leather, and had the building converted to a residence. Ernest F. Harris purchased the house in 1900, and sold it to John. P. Harris in 1908. At this time the front room was used as a barber shop, where Cronen Gray cut hair. In the back, Elias Price repaired harnesses and leather goods. It passed from Lorenzo and Elizabeth B. Norwood, to L. Pierce Bowlus, who bought it in 1921. He sold it to Edward L. and Carmye F. Norwood in 1937 who rented it to Sis and Doss Nicholson, and later Gabe and Carrie Burdette Burgee.

10. Singer Sewing Machine Building
lot 43

Levi Zeigler was an agent for the Singer Sewing Machine Co. in the 1870's. He had the office for his distributorship next to his house.

11. Zeigler House
lots 41, 42, 95, 96 & 97

Thomas Burgee, Jr. may have built a log house here first when he owned this property in 1820. David Zeigler added to the log house in 1850, after inheriting it from his wife's parents. David and Ann lived there until 1866, when they sold it to son Levi Zeigler for $600.00. Levi moved to the house after leaving the sawmill. Levi died 1901, and his son Ernest sold the house in 1902 to Charles Price and then Jasper and Edna Price. The house 2 1/2 story house has lapped and novelty clap boarding, The porch wraps from the east to north elevation, with a flat roof supported by metal posts. Two story south ell has a gabled roof with raised metal seam covering, black louvered shutters, adding charm to the street scene. The log beams under the house have L. C. Zeigler carved in them.

12. Bowman-Harris General Store
lot 40 south corner of Second Alley and Main Street

Site of Asa Hyatt's log house, 1820, later D. W. Dutrow's Mercantile which burned down. Peddlers could come to get re-outfitted at mercantiles such as this. Traveling salesmen [or drummers], carried their samples with them, and needed lodging, supper, and stable/livery facilities. Built in 1876, it was later converted into a residence in the 1930's, where Lucy and Edgar Burdette lived and ran a butcher shop in the back.

13. Hyattstown School
lot 94 on Second Alley at West Street

The lot was purchased from Levi C. Zeigler on 12 August 1878 for $100.00. On 19 Nov. 1878 the board approved $655.00 for the construction of the building, and furniture. This 24' by 26' two room school house replaced "Swamp College". It was completed and opened in 1880. The school at this time went up to the seventh grade. The school had double desks, where two children shared a bench style seat. They had ink wells and also had pencils (which cost a penny) and copybooks (which cost two cents). On 4 March 1881 this item appeared in the Sentinel: "The boys and girls of our town enjoyed on last Friday evening, defeating the Comus school in a spelling match. Whilst we can boast of our fine stores and churches, we must close our mouths when we think of our poor schools. Shame upon a School Board that recognizes spite work."

Teachers listed: John Shipley, Isaac Davis, W. W. Darby, James E. Duvall, Myra Wolfe, Forrest Gott, Miss Barry Albert, Viola Hunt, from Frostburg, who boarded with Nellie Burdette, Miss Margaret Devilbiss, Rev. Robert C. Lutton, Miss Powers, Mollie Green and Willis O. Rhodes. In 1900, John Darby, Jr. and Mrs. Maggie Ryan were both teaching. Mary Ryan, daughter of Maggie, then followed. Courtney Wade was the last teacher here before the school closed. Beginning in 1925, Jim Thompson drove a bus to Rockville High School daily for students who wished to continue their education.

Willis Rhodes had taught in Flagstaff, AZ before returning to Maryland to teach. He told many stories to the students about the wolves howling at night, and the landscape of the southwest. Mr. Rhodes was the only male teacher at the Kingley School before transferring to Hyattstown, in June of 1900. He also taught at Glen Echo. Mrs. Ryan, who taught the lower grades when Mr. Rhodes was teaching the upper grades, contracted tuberculosis, and eventually had to leave.

Richie Benson grew up in Hyattstown and attended the Hyattstown School. She says that there were two teachers at that time, Willis O. Rhodes and Viola Hunt. She usually walked home for lunch, and only carried one when the weather was bad. The teacher could fix a lunch on the pot belly stove for those who came from out lying areas, it was similar to gruel. At recess they played ante-over, a game where they threw a ball over the schoolhouse, and someone had to run and get it on the other side. Also, they played stick ball and did chin-ups on the bar between the trees. Frank Linthicum was on the school dodge ball team. When the students attended the county-wide field day at the old fairgrounds in Rockville, the Hyattstown dodge ball team competed in the tournament. Frank remembers that they made it to the finals and their opponent was "Froggy Hollow" school in Kingsley. The victorious team members from Hyattstown were awarded medals after the game. The school was auctioned in 1947, being purchased by A. R. Carlisle and subsequently turned into a private residence.

14. Christian Church Parsonage
lots 39 & 93

Site of the Lemuel Nicholson log house 1820, renovated, the Lottie Cecil house stood closer to the road than the present house at this location, in fact so close that the front porch practically was the sidewalk. Henrietta Benton bought the two lots from Lottie Cecil in 1879. William Lewis, wife Elizabeth and 3 children lived here c. 1898. In August of 1920, Bradley Hill Dudrow and his wife Birdie Beall Dudrow granted lot 39 to the Christian Church for the parsonage. The present parsonage is in the Colonial Revival style built on the site of the former garden located behind Mrs. Cecil's house. The parsonage was built in 1922 for $600.00.

15. Christian Church
lots 92 & 38

In 1820 lot 38 was owned by George Slacker. This lot was later sold to Jacob Thomas in 1826. To meet it's growing needs, the congregation decided to build a new structure on land donated by Jacob B. Thomas & wife, Elizabeth Ann Norwood, granddaughter of Eli Hyatt. In 1870 the cornerstone was laid under the leadership of Rev. Alfred N. Gilbert, and the present two-story building was completed for a cost of $3,000.00. The new building was dedicated 20 August, 1871 with a congregation of about 40 members. Levi C. Zeigler was elected elder and Thomas Price, Philip C. Dudrow, C. Harrison, and Luther Norwood, nephew of the donors of the land, were elected deacons. A formal deed was executed in 1876 when Elizabeth A. Norwood Thomas and Jacob Thomas granted unto Thomas Norwood, Andrew Hammon, Sr., Thomas Price, George W. Davis and Jacob Thomas, as trustees, for the "exclusive use for the Society of Christian people called Disciples of Christ residing in the vicinity of and in the habit of attending divine worship n the building commonly known as the Christian Church of Hyattstown. The congregation was incorporated on 3 May 1890 as the Hyattstown Christian Church, signed by the following officers of the church: Charles Price, Jacob Thomas, Thomas Norwood, William Horman, Thomas Price and Levi Christopher Zeigler. During this period, the church was heated by two wood stoves, one on each side of the sanctuary. The lighting was from coal lamps. Horses were tied to hitching posts out front. The bell was added in 1915. It was rung for services on Sundays, and at 11:00 each Armistice Day. The church held an annual Children's Day in June, Strawberry Festival in June and a church picnic in August. It was held at Mountain View Park from midday until dark. Music was provided by the Browningsville Band, with games, food, speeches and after electricity [c. 1925] cake walks. During September or October the church had two weeks of evangelistic services, with a prominent evangelist. The last Sunday would be the day for baptisms, at Bennett Creek, until 1920 when the baptistery was added, which was heated by a small stove-like heater. In 1920 two lots adjoining the church property were deeded to the Christian Church by Mr. and Mrs. Bradley H. Dudrow and used as the site of the new parsonage. The educational building with kitchen, hall, office, four classrooms, rest rooms and baptistery was built in 1954 at a cost of $13,500.00 and dedicated in June 1955. [parking lot is lot 38].

Ministers of the Christian Church:

1840	Robert Ferguson
	Neal McCollum
	John P. Mitchell
	William Schell
1890	Rev. Mr. Wolfe
	Alfred Gilbert
1912-19	Oliver C. Barnes
1920-22	Ralph V. Funk
1924-31	Robert Clifford Lutton
1931-40	Oliver C. Barnes
1940-42	Leslie Bowers
1942-44	G. D. Lamb
1944-52	Ladue B. McGill
1953-55	J. Arthur Mott
1956	Charles H. Funk
1956-57	Maitland Watterworth
1957-63	J. Arthur Mott
1963	Gerald Flinn
1964-68	Albert H. Tisdall
1968-72	Theodore Keckler
1972-76	David L. Watterworth
1976-83	John S. Powell
1983-84	Caren Cullen-Knapp
1984	W. F. Terry Reister

16. Stella Miles House
lots 37 & 91

Site of Ralph Norwood's house, this was later the site of the Mr. Harris's garage. Around 1945 Stella Miles had Raymond Spring build an addition and renovate it for her house.

17. Jacob Thomas House
lots 36 & 90

Barrick Hall owned these lots in 1820 with a log house on lot 36. Later a frame two-story addition with a long porch was added. The house was much deeper than the front section that faced the road. The one story porch was trimmed with bric a brac and supported by four six faceted columns on the front, and six down the side porch. The house was L shaped and was painted yellow. At the end of the side porch was a swing and lattice, with a pump behind that. Will and Minnie Dutrow lived here for many years. After this house was abandoned the fire department burned it as a training exercise.

18. Davis-Tabler House
lots 35 & 89

George Davis bought this lot and had a house built in 1809. The house was built of Flemish bond bricks, made on the property, and has had several styles of front porches. It had a separate kitchen building, which was later joined to the back of the house. It sold to Daniel Collins, the first Constable and also a tailor. He learned his trade while studying for the priesthood in New York, but after being de-frocked came to Hyattstown. He was fined for accepting illegal fees from Jesse Hyatt in Equity Court, and left for the Great Falls area in 1818. Joseph Anderson purchased the house and sold it in 1850 to Nicholas Worthington, a wealthy merchant, who lived there with his wife and daughter. In 1863 Zerviah McElfresh bought the property for $ 1,000 from Nicholas Worthington. In 1866 Levi Price bought it from William L. Grimes and wife. Levi Price was the owner and operator of Price's Distillery, just outside of town. From 1868-1910 Jacob and Mary Tabler lived in the house. Jake Tabler was proud of his participation in the War as a Union Army Captain and of being a veteran of Gettysburg. He flew the flag from his porch and dressed in his Army uniform on special occasions. The photo taken in 1907 shows Mr. Tabler in his Union dress uniform. In the years following, Charles Tabler lived here. He was a carpenter and his daughter, Catherine, was a dressmaker. In 1911 Carl and Nellie A. Burdette moved from across the street, into the brick house. Nellie purchased it in 1915. She lived the back rooms, and rented the front rooms to travelers, teachers, and boarders.

Davis-Tabler House

19. Brengle-Burdette House
lots 33, 34, 87 & 88

In 1803 these four lots were sold to 2 brothers: Eli Brashears and Dr. Belt Brashears. They soon built a one-story log house where James Hinton lived. They advertised in the <u>Frederick Town Herald</u> 1804: "for sale or rent by Brashears." The house was enlarged before 1820 to a two-story log house. In 1831 the lots were sold to Daniel Price for $250. In 1850 Price lost the lots at a Constable sale for taxes. In 1851 the four lots were purchased by Nicholas Worthington for $400.00 the house may have been deteriorated by then and lost value. In 1864 C. Thomas Anderson bought all four lots. He was a carpenter, blacksmith, churn maker and had been awarded a patent in 1861 for his new churn design. He added to the dwelling, enlarging the rear and added porch.

In 1865 Anderson sold the property to Ursula Brengle, widow of Lewis Tabler for $800.60. Ursula's second husband, John H. Brengle was a buggymaker, carriage maker, painter and decorator. He installed the German siding and added the Victorian trim of the day: jigsaw bric a brac. In 1892 the property was sold to Marietta Koehler. In 1897 John Burdette, harness and saddle maker, purchased the property. George W. Murphy was living here when he died in 1915. Willie Lloyd Burdette, first "mayor" of Hyattstown then lived in the house where he raised his family.

20. Smith-Darby House
lots 31-32, 85-86

William Brewer bought lots 31 and 32 for speculation from Jesse Hyatt in 1800 for $70.00 In 1806 Charles McElfresh bought the property and six years later constructed a house, adding lots 85 & 86 to the property. In 1824 McElfresh sold them to Philemon M. Smith, Sr. for $800.00. From 1824-1878 the Smith Family lived there. The present home was built about 1840 in the Federal style, with the wing added in 1853. The small frame shed in the rear of the house served as the post office from 1849 until 1853. In 1862 N. Joshua Hatcher married Sarah Riggs Hyatt, a daughter of Jesse Hyatt. Dr. Hatcher may have been the first to practice medicine here, beginning in 1865. From 1880-1883 Dr Asa H. Zeigler, used the wing on south end of house for his office. Next, Dr. Ransone lived there and also practiced dentistry here. When Dutrow Linthicum came in with a tooth ache, Dr. Ransone accidentally pulled the wrong tooth, so he put it back in and pulled the on next to it. His widow and children are listed here in the 1900 Census, and a shown as owning the house. In recent years Robert Clifton Darby owned this home. His wife, Ethel Cecil Darby lived there for 40+ years. Currently, the

Wilkinson family is restoring the house. It is a 2 1/2 story Flemish bond brick house with a roofed porch supported by five square wooden posts with decorative scroll work at the top. The two-story addition was built of common bonded brick. The property includes a latticed pump enclosure, carriage shed and iron fence in the back. Also a grape arbor and root cellar, used for storing vegetables. The house has a gable and shed roof covered by corrugated red tin. This impressive house is a landmark in Hyattstown.

21. Minerva Dudrow House
lot 30

This mid-19th Century frame building was remodeled in the Victorian style. It was the home of Philip and Acshah Dudrow and their son Bradley Hill Dudrow was born here. Will and Minnie Dudrow also lived here. Later, it was sold to the Byron and Georgie Dudrow Darby. Byron Darby had numerous bee hives out back and sold strained honey, honey comb and eggs on a roadside stand. Byron worked for Bradley Dudrow and eventually became his partner. Georgie grew dahlias, and had a friendly running competition with her sister-in-law, Birdie Dudrow.

22. Gardner Carpenter Shop/Lyles House
lots 29 and 83

This structure originally was a shop for the Gardner family business. After being converted to a residence, Henry, Sarah, Henry Jr., Russell, Suc, and Virgie Lyles lived here. Virgie was the local mid-wife and took in laundry. The local children enjoyed gathering mulberries and eating cookies while visiting "Aunt Sarah."

23. Gardner House
lots 28 and 82

Built partly of log before the Civil War, this two-story house is
now protected by siding. John Gardner, the carpenter and
undertaker, lived here. The school teacher, Willis Rhodes,
lived here, before moving to the cabin across the road. Later it
was owned by Ella May Grimes Gardner, who boarded guests.
Edgar and Lizzie Burdette lived there and then Zach Windsor
and his mother lived here in the 1930's. Miss Frances Maher
lived here and ran a curiosity shop next door after that time.

24. MP Church South

Jacob R. Tabler and wife Mary granted to John Lewis, Charles Harding, Edward Grafton Gardner, E. Edward Lewis, Warner Welsh, F. L. Windsor and the board of Trustees a lot across from the ME Church to be used, kept, maintained and disposed of as a place of divine worship for the use of the ministry and membership of the Methodist Church South Dec. 1874. The first steward was William B. Lewis. The frame gothic revival church was completed in 1876, the building costing $1,200.00. Sunday School Superintendents include W. W. Welsh and Edward Norwood. Horace Thompson was the Treasurer, and Roxye Norwood taught Sunday School here before the churches were re-united in 1939. The building was sold in 1952 to Frances Maher.

Pastors of the MP Church:
1866-67 John P. Hall
1867-68 Robert Smith, R. Wilson
1868-69 F. C. Tebbs
1869-73 Benjamin F. Ball
1873-75 W. A. McDonald, A. C. McNeer
1875-77 William A. Wade, L. L. Lloyd
1877-78 M. A. Gaver, M. P. Scanlon
1878-79 M. A. Gaver, S. F. Butts
1879-80 W. W. Watts, D. F. Eutzler
1880-81 W. W. Watts, J. C. Graichen
1881-82 W. W. Watts, John Miller
1882-83 W. W. Watts, C. W. Mark
1883-85 J. H. Boyd
1885-86 J. H. Boyd, J. H. Kuhlman
1886-87 J. H. Boyd, E. L. Gies
1887-89 Will G. Hammond, D. L. Blakemore
1889-90 Will G. Hammond, W. L. Smith
1890-91 A. P. Neel, D. M. Henderson
1891-94 William E. Wolfe, Will G. Hammond
1894-96 J. H. Dulany, C. P. Smith
1896-99 W. H. Sanders, G. W. Bagle
1900-01 D. L. Reid

1901-05 I. G. Michael
1905-07 W. C. Smith, J. L. Dulany
1907-08 H. L. Bivens
1909-10 E. T. Caton
1913-14 J. T. Mitchell
1914-16 W. C. Smith
1916-22 G. R. Mays
1922-26 H. L. Coffman
1926-28 J. E. McDonald
1928-30 C. L. Reiter
1930-32 E.W. Jordan
1932-36 S. J. L. DuLaney

25. site of Walter Lawson House
shopping center

Built in 1920, the Colonial Revival frame house with red trim, hip roof, front porch extended across the front of the house, barn in rear. Tourist cabins were built in 1938 by Mr. Lawson and called "Orchard Inn.". They were converted in stages in the late 1960's to duplex apartments. House was built for Edgar and Lucy Burdette, but sold to William and Noble Lawson in 1933. The family lived there until it was sold to Thomas E. & Margaret M. Burnett who sold it for the current shopping center.

McElfresh Burying Ground

The cemetery is located off of Fire Tower Road on the former McElfresh farm. Many of the original settlers graves are located here. The haven trees growing here were brought from China for the silkworm industry which was started in the mid-1830's.

Manions diner and filling station was located near the Mountain View Park and Carnival Grounds. Annie Manion ran the restaurant and a concession stand in the summer. Vernon Manion built a cottage for his sister Helen to live at the top of the hill after she contracted tuberculosis.

26. The Mountain View Park

The park was a popular spot for jousting tournaments, ballgames, church picnics, speeches, reunions, band concerts and had a dance pavilion. Montgomery Sentinel July 4, 1872: "At an early hour in the morning, the beauty of the village was astir and the roads were seen filled in all directions with vehicles bringing their precious freight to view the manly sport of presence of encouragement to the brave knights there assembled to thrust a lance in defense of female honor and virtue. Successful knights were awarded an honor of crowning the queen of love and beauty." Montgomery Sentinel Aug. 20 1904: "Picnic for the benefit of the baseball team will be held at Tabler's Grove near Hyattstown Wednesday 31 Aug beginning 10:00 AM there will be dinner, games, etc. Frederick Select Orchestra will play and a platform will be erected for dancing." Fire Department Dinners were held here, with the Ladies Auxiliary preparing the food. Tickets were sold from an old black buggy. Each year during the carnival, a parade was held which begun near the mill road, and marched to the top of the hill. Majorettes, local bands and a Grand Marshall were featured. The carnival had rides and booths were set up, with games and food.

27. Home of Eli Hyatt

Called "The Red House" this farm was for sale in 1825 after his death, listed as a two-story large frame house. The house has two main sections, and the one-story front porch is supported by four posts. The back porch has two-stories. The north section of the house, a typical center gable Maryland farm house, had several additions on it. The farm was later known as the Tabler farm.

28. Burdette Garage

This lot was originally owned by Eli Wolfe, but more recently was the site of filling station and garage run by E. Dolston Burdette, after he left the Burdette Brothers.

29. Methodist Episcopal Church

The present church was built by local contractor John Gardner in 1856. The original floor was white oak. After a termite infestation, the floor was replaced with concrete. The second story balcony was removed and the Greek Revival brick edifice has been stuccoed. Plasterer Jim Manion did the pebblestone stucco work after 1939. The altar and pews were installed in 1955 and were made by the Cavetown Milling Co. The addition behind altar was added in 1959 for classroom space. The commemorative windows were created in 1955. Frank Linthicum remembers going to K Street in Washington, DC to pick them up and have them installed. Annie Miles Linthicum played the organ here for 60 years, and her sister Louise Thompson sometimes substituted for her. Some of the Sunday School teachers were Sam Miles, Roxye Norwood Anderson, Laura Cecil Walker, Marian Cecil Miles, and Rachel Linthicum. The members attended the campmeetings in Browningsville each summer. The Mission Society was renamed The Ladies Aid Society. Mrs. Leona Linthicum was the president for many years, followed by her daughter, Kitty Linthicum, who was president for 30 years. This was the forerunner of the United Methodist Women. Directly behind the church is the Methodist Cemetery where the stones of many Hyattstown settlers can be seen and on the north side of the church is the Hyattstown Community Cemetery.

Pastors of the Hyattstown ME/UM Church:
1828-30 Enoch George
1830-32 Beverly Waugh
1832-34 Alfred Griffith
1834-36 Frederick Stier
1836-38 Hamilton Jefferson
1838-40 Jesse Lee
1840-42 Christopher Fry
1842-44 James Paintey

1844-46 Tobias Riley
1846-48 Thomas Larkin
1848-50 Job Gees
1850-52 Caleb Reynolds
1852-54 Basil Barny
1854-56 Andrew Hemphill
1856-58 L. D. Herron, Rev. Langley, Charles A. Reed,
   G. R. Jefferson
1858-60 Samuel Cornelius, William E. Magruder
1860-63 J. L. Gilbert, A. B. Dolly
1863-64 S. V. Leech, R. W. O. Metzger, C. H. Mytinger
1864 -66 Rev W. J. Holliday
1866-67 J. W. Start, E. E. Shipley
1867-68 J. W. Start, G. W. Hobbs
1868-69 J. D. Still, G. W. Hobbs
1869-70 J. D. Still, D. M. Browning
1871-74 Harrison McNemar
1874-77 T. Marshall West
1877-80 Emory Burhman
1880-83 Randolph Richardson Murphy
1883-86 W. R. Gwinn, A. H. Thompson, assistant
1886-90 Thomas J. Cross, A. H. Thompson, assistant
1890-92 J. R. Pardew
1892-94 W. F. Roberts
1894-96 J. W. Steele
1896-99 William Harris
1899-02 Elmer E. Marshall
1902-11 Caleb M. Yost
1911-16 Thomas S. Davis
1916-17 Walter S. Jones
1917-20 Frank Y. Jaggers
1920-26 Wallace M. Brashears
1926-30 W. E. Nelson
1930-35 Fred R. Barnes
1935-40 Hartwell F. Chandler
1940-42 Ira W. Shindle
1942-45 W. D. Shindle
1945-47 E. K. Sawyers
1947-53 Don E. Griffin

1953-56 Ernest L. Harrison
1956-58 William T. Miller
1958-63 Hayden L. Sparks
1963-68 Richard C. Johnson
1968-80 James E. Chance
1980-90 Lynn D. Cairns
1990-92 Gaye Smith
1992-97 Phillip Ayers
1997-   James Miller

30. Miles House
lots 27 & 81

This one-story frame house with front porch was built in 1937 for Samuel Miles. It had two bedrooms, a kitchen and living room. In the back was a chicken brooder house, privy, and shed In 1947 the porch was enclosed, and the pump converted to running water. A stairway was added in the bedroom leading to the floored attic. During this same time period an oil burning heater was added in the basement. It was sold to the Methodist Church for Sunday School classes and MYF by their granddaughter, Elizabeth Miles Burdette.

31. Anderson House
lots 26 & 80

White frame house of Pearl and John Anderson, Jr. was built c. 1942 by Webster Burdette. Wayne Hawes now lives here.

lot 24 site of Dudrow's blacksmith shop c. 1879-1900.

32. Anderson-Linthicum House
lots 23 & 77

Site of Otho W. and Amanda P. Duyrow House, c. 1835. In
1912, Helen Murphy Richards was living there with her children. This house burned down. the present house was built in
1926 for John L. and Edie Anderson by Webster Burdette.
The house is a shingle style bungalow, and was the home of
Frank and Violet Linthicum. Recently remodeled by Rick
Wagner.

33. Wolfe-Cecil House
lots 21 & 75 on Third Alley North East corner

Built around 1810, the two oldest sections of the house are of
log construction. Levi Phillips owned this 1850's. In 1859 Eli
Wolfe sold this property to John Gardner. The house was
remodeled after Edward Grafton Gardner acquired it in 1862.
He was a local contractor, builder, cabinet maker, and manufacturer of coffins. There is also a stable/shed of frame
construction in the back; both have stone foundations. In 1917
John Gardner, heir of E. G. Gardner, sold the property to
Humphrey D. Wolfe, who sold it in 1934 to William Cecil. In
1955 it was sold to Arbus & Phyllis Jones, who sold it in 1975
to Joseph J. and Donna L. Zetts. The middle and rear ell
section is 1 1/2 stories, made of logs with two rooms down-
stairs, and two upstairs.

34. School
lot 74 at Third Alley and East Street

Along Third Alley was the school "Swamp College." Ownership of lot 74 transferred from Mary Ann Hyatt/Ann Welsh/Charles O. Peters/Lucy Pyles and then for $ 350.00 to Floyd Horine. Montgomery County purchased one lot from the Welsh's for Hyattstown to build a school. It was bounded by on the North by the Gardner property, on the East by the branch, on the South by the Welsh property, and West by Welsh's garden. The school stood 250 feet east of the public highway in a low marshy spot of land on wood lots. The school was familiarly named "Swamp College." There were about a dozen houses comprising Hyatt's Town then. In 1831, the first school term, students attended the frame structure, with six windows, and had only one half the size of the later school house. There were straight backed benches long enough to seat many students on one bench and few pictures or maps. Students in grades one through eight attended classes here which included being taught to read by the ABC's method, and math by the numbers instead of combinations. The schoolhouse served 60-70 students and was organized 30 years prior to county-wide public education. Thomas Hill was the second teacher, 19 years old at the time and boarding with Philp Dudrow. In 1861 he enlisted in the US Army. Bradley Hill Dudrow was named for him.

Other teachers were: M. Wellington Welsh who lived to be 98, his brother, Turner Welsh (finest disciplinarian in the history of the school), Bob Berlton, Frank Welsh, Lizzie Viers, Forest Prettyman, Jim Burns, J. Benjamin Hodges [paid $58.00 for the term] J. Windsor Hodges (1860-7), Charles E. Hill (who also taught alternating terms at Woodfield) and Mary Miller from Staunton, VA. She enjoyed organizing programs held in the schoolroom at night by the light of coal oil lamps. These functions were attended be people as far away as Frederick, who drove down by horse and buggy. Some outstanding students were: Robert Layton-later a physician, Charles Vall, Willis O. Rhodes, later a teacher. Two of the oldest pupils were Grafton Gardner b. 1832 and Andrew Jackson Tabler.

It was a general custom to "turn the teacher out" on Christmas Eve. The boys would lock the teacher out when s/he walked home for lunch. The students would stay inside until the teacher gave up-thus giving the teacher and pupils a half day holiday. The teacher enjoyed this prank as much as the students did. The mischief was not only confined to Christmas Eve. One day Dorsey Gardner turned loose a squirrel during the school hours and the children had a merry chase all over the room, as the students tried to catch "friend squirrel."

Mr. Welsh chased Katie Welsh around the school-room for some misdemeanor, until she ran out the door and home to the mill. Mr. Welsh lost the race. The old school and lot were sold back to the Welsh family as it became inadequate for the growing community and was unpleasantly located. The first request for a new school was tabled by the board on November 12, 1876 for lack of funds. The school closed in 1880.

35. Horine House
lot 20 & 74

This house was built in 1934 by Webster V. Burdette for Floyd Horine on lot 20. It is a square Colonial Revival with hip roof, German siding, full length front porch, and has nice hardwood trim inside. Currently the home of Don Burgess.

36. site of Jackson Cabin
lot 19 & 73

George Jackson had a cabin on lot 19 by 1820. The foundation of the cabin is all that remains. The cabin stood until 1973 when it was disassembled and moved to Waterford, Virginia. It had passed from Mary Ann Hyatt, who left it to Ann Welsh, then to Warner Wellington Welsh in 1889. He sold it to Charles Peters, who sold it to Lucinda Pyles. Teacher Willis Rhodes lived here at one time. Irene Lusby and her family later lived here. In 1924 Edward Heffner, heir and brother of Lucinda Pyles, sold it to Minerva C. R. Horine, widow of Edwin M. Horine.

37. The Hyatt House
lots 18, 17, 71 & 72

This land was purchased from Jesse Hyatt in 1803 & 1807 by Jacob Smith who built the main section of the house, one of 12 standing in 1811. In 1816 he sold it to Henry Ramseller, Sr. for $900.00. In 1818 Levi Phillips bought the house and also 22 other lots in Hyatt's Town. Phillip's son-in-law, Asa Hyatt, a merchant, and his wife Mary Ann Phillips Hyatt moved into the Hyatt House before 1845, when James K. Polk was a guest. The hotel was conveyed to the grandchildren of Asa & Mary Ann and widower Warner W. Welsh--his sons converted the building into a general store and residence (with Post Office) and lived there until 1890. The building continued as a store until 1919. It was the Price Family residence after that time. In the 1885 inventory of Warner Welsh's store, numerous items are listed with their price. It is interesting to see that diverse items, from violin strings to diaper pins, and fish hooks to candles were available. A parasol listed for $1.75 while a ream of paper was $2.25. A box of hair dye was .33, while shoes were $1.05. Mousetraps, tonics, buttons, and many gadgets are also listed.

38. Welsh - Jamison House
lots 16 & 70

This two-story frame house is typical of the 19th Century architecture. The Welsh family lived here until 1890 Warner Welsh's heirs sold it to Richard H. and Elizabeth Bowman. They rented the house to John Darby, the school teacher. Mr. Rhodes lived there in 1914. Helen Richards lived there, followed by the Browning family. In 1919, Robert V. Price and Lucy M. bought the house from the heirs of the Bowmans. The house then passed from Robert V. Price to Ben F. Price in 1931, to Cornelius R. Comegy, in 1943 and later, Mildred Horman lived here. Currently this is the home of the Jamisons.

39. Dutrow-Price House
lots 14, 15, 68 and Second Alley

Rezin Hobb's log house of 1805 was expanded by 1852. It later became the George Grimes shoeshop and residence, by combining the structures in an L-shape. The house passed to Daniel William Dutrow, who had his store across the road. Mrs. Annie Leather and Frank later lived here. Gabe and Stella Lawson rented the house before Eugene Murphy and his family lived here, followed by Jack and Lou Kinna Price.

40. Murphy House
lots 13 & 67

Luther Watkins sold the property to Attie Lee Watkins who sold to Charles Basil Murphy in 1911 for $1150.00. In the 1940's Mrs. Murphy rented rooms and allow her grandchildren to have their Hyattstown friends over for taffy pulls, playing spin the bottle, and to square dance. Dancing was frowned on, so she'd pull down the blinds. At 9 PM she would walk into the living room winding the alarm clock, which was everyone's signal that it was time to go home. The Murphy house had a pump that gave delicious cold mountain water. On the back porch was a swing, and a grape vine. The grandchildren took a Saturday night bath in a small washtub standing up, to get ready for church the next morning. The parlor was only used for special occasions, such as funerals and the door was kept closed. Mrs. Murphy's daughter-in-law would take off her high heeled shoe to kill the chicken for Sunday dinner. "She would put it's neck between the heel and toe, and then whack him." The Murphy heirs sold to Perry Hipkins in 1956. Presently the Jewell residence.

41. Norwood-Anderson House
Lot 12 & 66

This two-story home was constructed prior to 1890. Widow Mary Anderson and her daughter Ella, a dressmaker, lived here prior to Edward and Carmye Norwood who moved here in 1912. Ed worked at B. H. Dudrow's store. Their daughter Roxye and husband, Clifton Anderson, a local produce huckster lived here for many years in recent times.

42. site of the Webster Burdette House
lots 9 & 63

Old brick house, with some Victorian trim such as barge boards and four chimneys. The large English basement was a cool place to go in the summer. This house had a two-story front porch and a one-story side porch. Mr. Web Burdette moved there from Clarksburg in 1914. He remodeled this house and several others in the community.

43. Lillie Stone House
lots 7 & 61

This once beautiful home has a slate roof, probably from the Hyattstown Quarry. The two-story frame house was built in the mid 1860's and featured two main rooms on each floor. The kitchen was added later by Web Burdette. Due to termites, the house was covered with asbestos siding, in the 1920's.

44. Campanaro's
lot 5

Site of the Post Office, this building now houses the barber shop, restaurant and upstairs apartments.

45. Bradley Hill Dudrow General Store
lot 5

Later called "Dudrow and Darby's" Bradley Hill Dudrow usually left his store unlocked. If you needed something when a clerk was not there, you signed for the merchandise in his book. In the store, the post office was located in the back, a pot-bellied stove was in the middle, a barber's chair was available, a large glass case of candy was near the front and there was a pickle barrel. Local children enjoyed selecting candy from the case and watching Mr. Dudrow bag the penny candy, and then wind string from a large spool around the bag. Later, he also sold ice cream and Esso gasoline.

Dudrow's Store

46. Burdette Brothers
lot 4

Site of a small log house, owned by Will Price, and rented to tenants. Later, Willie Lloyd and Dolston Burdette started their business here. The garage opened in 1919 and is a landmark in Hyattstown. It is now covered in brick veneer. It became a Chevrolet dealer in 1927, and several additions have been made since that time. Over the garage was a hall used by the townsfolk for Halloween parties, dinners, plays, and box socials.

47. Site of Tan yard
lots 1, 2, 52, 53, 54, 106 & 107

Founded in 1825 by Lewis Tabler, the tannery comprised 2 1/3 acres of land. Hides from local herds were soaked in sumac, and dipped in tannin made from the bark of local oak trees. The tannery had a bark shed, a flesher shed, engine house and 18 dipping vats with water powered by a dam and water way coming from Little Bennett Creek. The process had an unpleasant odor and polluted the local creek. Hides were then sent to a currier, who prepared the leather for the saddlemaker, shoemaker, coachmaker and bookbinder. Abraham died in 1868 and his sons William and Abraham Tabler continued running the tannery for a short time. Creditors brought suit against brother Andrew Jackson Tabler-administrator of the will. The Volunteer Fire Department was founded in 1928, one of the first in Montgomery County. The first president was Webster Burdette. The first chief was Willie Lloyd Burdette. Three of the charter members were: Jesse C. Rippeon, Edwin Dolston Burdette, and Clifton Anderson. It was built on the former tannery site. Annual Fireman's Supper's, held in the hall above the station draw folks from as far away as Washington, DC.

ANNUAL FIREMAN'S SUPPER
Country Ham, Oysters and Turkey
★ **SATURDAY, MARCH 9, 1968** ★

Beginning at 3:00 p.m.
AT THE
★ HYATTSTOWN FIRE HALL ★
BENEFIT
HYATTSTOWN VOLUNTEER FIRE DEPARTMENT

Adults $2.00   Carry Outs .25 Extra   Children $1.00

---

48. Blacksmith Shop
lot 55

Albert Phillips' smithy was located across from the mill, site of present stone wall structure. Subsequent smithy's who were located here include: Frank Mortimer and Pete Smith. Charles Luhn's wheelwright shop was adjacent to Philip's Smithy.

49. Feed and Flour Mill

At the time of the town's founding, the miller was George Wolfe. Sr., who had taken over the mill when William Richards died. Mr. Wolfe purchased the mill seat in 1807 and sold the property to Benjamin Waters and Frederick Baker for $5,000 in 1814. Baker operated the mill for 10 years after taking sole possession, until 1827 when he sold to Otho Norris and wife, Sarah. They sold the property to William Farrer, who made substantial improvements to the mill over the next five years. It was a two-run flour mill and saw mill, with one employee and an output of 6,000 bushels of meal & 35,000 feet of lumber annually, valued at $4,125.00.

In 1858 William Farrer advertised the property for sale, intending to move from the area. The published advertisement in the <u>Montgomery Sentinel</u>: October 8, 1858 lists a re-built mill with new burrs, and a group of connected buildings, 25 acres of land, with a large, frame dwelling house, one small dwelling house, one flouring mill, 2 pair of four feet burr, new, and all of the latest improvements for a merchant mill. One country mill, 1 pair of 3 feet 7 inch burrs all new machinery, one saw mill connected with the merchant and country mill. The term merchant or flouring mill refers to two runs of stone usually reserved for the grinding of wheat. While the country mill would be ordinarily used for custom grinding or for grinding corn. All it appears was housed in one building.

George A. Darby purchased the mill seat in 1872, for $2,901.00. The 1880 Census lists Darby as the owner, with one assistant. He operated the mill until 1905, when he sold it to John W. Harris, who made improvements to the mill, by installing a new roller mill replacing the stone, adding a steam boiler and engine and an inside and outside corn shelter beneath a shed roof. Charles Basil Murphy was the miller when Mr. Harris owned the mill. He sold the mill in 1911 to Bradley Hill Dudrow, who had many business ventures and purchased it only for an investment. He sold the mill in 1912 to Mortimer and Luhn. Ruth Mortimer Price recalls playing in the bran piles beside the mill. In the barn across the way they kept two horses, and a milk cow; the loft was for storing hay. In 1914 Charles Russell Murphy began grinding for Frank Mortimer and Charles Luhn. Mortimer was a machinist (mechanical engineer) formerly with Baldwin Locomotive Co, Philadelphia. Luhn was a carriage maker, cabinet maker and wheelwright. Both did their work while financing milling operation making the mill a small scale industrial park. The mill handled the grinding of some grains and cereals, buckwheat coming predominantly from the Purdum-Lewisdale area. Winter wheat, yellow and white corn were the principle grains milled here. Most of the grain was purchased outright, but some custom grinding continued--crushed for food or toll grinding; so called because the miller retained 25% of the finished product as a grinding fee. The whole wheat flour, baker's flour, and corn meal were marketed locally in neighborhood stores, transported from the mill in a truck. The mill also marketed a small amount of self-rising flour which was produced by mixing baking powder with wheat flour. A small amount of marketing was done in the Frederick County area.

Montgomery Sentinel August 29, 1918: fire from overheated steamboiler consumed the building igniting corn cobs. Mortimer and Luhn had little capital--the new mill was to be built the least expensive method possible. Mr. Web Burdette

97

supervised the construction. At the time of the fire, the mill had 1,000 barrels of wheat inside, they never determined if it was spontaneous combustion or not. The community pitched in to help rebuild the mill and the wives cooked for the men working.

The metal water wheel was shipped to Hanover, PA for repairs. The warehouse of Price's Distillery, was purchased by by Mortimer and Luhn, dismantled and incorporated in the new mill. A run of burr stones and mill works were taken from a mill in Browningsville formerly owned and operated by Frank Gladhill. During the 1920's larger mills (Selby's in Germantown and Bowman's in Rockville) had an advantage of being located near the railroad and totally overpowered the Hyattstown Mill. The larger mills had the capacity to produce bleached flour, the most popular type which the smaller mills didn't handle, thus making their products more desirable and marketable. Mortimer and Luhn sold to Theodore Lenivitz in 1928. Although the property passed through many hands during the ensuing decades of the 20th Century the mill continued operating and was acquired for park purposes about 1970 by the National Capital Park and Planning Commission.

GRIST MILL,
HYATTS TOWN, MD.

50. Cronen Gray House

Listed as distillery worker in the 1900 census, his wife took in laundry. She had large black kettles and made her own soap. Her daughter, Mary, lived here with her common law husband, Pete Smith, who was a blacksmith. This house has been gone since 1965. House was frame two-story with center gable, and front porch.

51. Slate Quarry

The Hyattstown Slate Quarry is located off Old Hundred Road west of town. The Slate Quarry Road connects 109 to Thurston Road. About three quarters of the way down that road on the left is the remains of the quarry. Slate was obtained from this source as early as 1807 when a contract to supply roofing for the Capitol building was issued. When the source of funds ran out, the quarry closed down. Then in 1903 a new source was secured. Men began building dams to hold water for a power source when new machinery was ordered. The slate was used in the road projects in the area, as well as for roofing materials. By 1904 35 men were employed in the quarry. Boys from the Peach Bottom Quarry gained employment at the Hyattstown Quarry with the intention of sabotaging their competition. They dynamited the slate in such a way as to make the quarry no longer profitable.

52. Christian Cemetery

This site was also the original site of the Christian Church. The members who comprised the Christian Church of Hyattstown began meeting prior to 1830. They met in members homes, and when Alexander Campbell came through the area on a preaching tour in March 1834, he visited with the group. A product of the "Great Awakening" the Disciples of Christ, or Christians, combined a Presbyterian heritage with Methodist doctrines and Baptist policy and practice. This characteristic explains why Hyattstown Christian Church is listed as Baptist on the Martinet and Bond Map. William E. Anderson donated 3/4 of an acre of the "Resurvey on Wildcat Spring" to the Trustees for the building of the church, April 29, 1837. William McClenahan, Eli Wolfe, William Richards, Jr., and Josiah Wolfe, trustees. For erecting a "house of worship for the use of the congregation of Christians." The log meeting house was located on the old Frederick Road, just slightly northeast of the present cemetery. Charter members included: Lavinia Hyatt-Richards-Wolfe, Eli Wolfe, George Wolfe, Jr., Mary Davis Wolfe, Sarah Hyatt, David & Eleanor Zeigler, William Richards, Jr. & Charlotte Hyatt-Fowler-Richards, Thomas & Ann Sibley, George & Elizabeth Davis, Ann & Augustus Horman, Rachel & Eli Davis, William Anderson and his daughter, Eula Harris. Robert H. Ferguson was called to preach on the Rockville Circuit in 1840. This included Gunpowder, Rockville and Hyattstown. The first Elders of the organized church were Eli Wolfe and William Richards, Jr. The members of the congregation were baptized in the Bennett Creek, by immersion.

53. Zeigler Saw & Bone Mill

Christopher Zeigler owned and operated the sumac mill located on Little Bennett Creek. Zeigler's sumac mill had six employees and $1,000 capital investment in 1850. The mill was powered by a horse and three mules which ground 130 tons annually, worth $4,900 in the 9 month season. The extract was used at the tannery for dying hides. The property passed to his son David A. Zeigler and wife, Eleanor Ann Hyatt Zeigler who operated a saw and bone mill at the site. Local timber was turned into lumber and the bone mill yielded fertilizer for the local farmers use. Traces of the wheel pit and mill race are still visible at the mill site off Prescott Road.

54. Zeigler Log House

Originally the home of Christopher and Ann Zeigler, later, according to the 1850 Census, the Zeigler family operated a restaurant and inn at this site. The location proved to be a convenient one for people travelling on the Great Road, having either just made it up "Long Hill" or stopping for the night before attempting their descent. This was also their residence, up the hill from their mill. For protection from the elements, the house is presently covered in siding.

55. Montgomery Chapel

Founded in 1870 on land given by George and Martha Butler. The structure was brought in 1884, being a one room frame building. It stood on the east side of the Great Road 1 mile south of Hyattstown and was for blacks in the area. It also served as the schoolhouse until 1936. Attendance was frequently too low for a teacher, the state law requiring over 15 students. Although the church is no longer standing, the cemetery is still visible. George Butler is among those buried there. The church was on the Boyd's charge and was part of the Washington conference. It closed in December of 1963 because it did not meet county fire regulations, and was burned by the fire department. The members merged with John Wesley Church in 1964. The property went to the John Wesley Church for additional burial space.

MINISTERS OF MONTGOMERY CHAPEL

1886- 88	**William P. Ryder**
1889-91	**J. W. Galloway**
1892	**W. H. Brooks**
1892-95	**B. F. Myers**
1895-97	**Edward Moore**
1889-99	**B. B. Snowden**
1899-02	**Daniel Wheeler**
1902-03	**Bosley Boyce**
1906-09	**Nathan Ross**
1909-12	**J. S. Cole**
1913-16	**Rev. Lawson**
1917-18	**William E. Jefferson**
1919-20	**J. W. Langford**
1920-21	**W. P. Hopkins**
1921-23	**C. A. Randall**
1924-25	**J. H. Kent**
1925-35	**J. W. Lewis**
1935-38	**Melvin Johnson**
1938-39	**Robert B. Smith**
1939-40	**H. J. McDonald**
1940-53	**C. E. O. Smallwood**
1953-59	**J. W. Langford**
1959-62	**Joseph Stemley**
1962-64	**Clifton W. Aukward**

1961 New Year's Poem by Mrs. Wilson

A Happy New Year, to friends, and to neighbors.
Let the North and the South sheath their swords, and the sabers.
A Happy New Year, to Mamie and Ike
In just a few weeks they can do as they like.
And Greetings sincere to Dick and to Pat,
Very soon on the shelf, they can park the top hat.
Fond Greetings to lodge, and to brave Helen Keller,
But this year, no greetings to Nel Rockefeller.
And Greetings most cool to the Washington starlings,
I hope they won't visit us here, little--Darlings!
A salute to the roadmen, with sand trucks and cinders,
who work, to keep cars, from smashing to flinders.
To the milkman, who comes, though "no work", and "no school",
Through snow, sleet, and storm, with cream for our gruel.
To send Greetings to Kruschev and Castro, is whacky!
If we say, Happy New Year to Jack and to Jackie,
There are sisters galore, and Caroline loquacious,
It is well that the White House is roomy and spacious.
There is young baby John, and Peet-ah, the actor,
And Frankie Sinatra will be quite a factor.
Father Joe, Mother Rose, with French gown and frill.
And all of their kinfolk, and ALL Beacon Hill.
And Teddy who harbors a Senatorial hobby.
And of course, in the spot-light, there's young brother Bobby.
Like naming the Roosevelts, it would take the whole year
If the Kennedy Tribe, I should try to name here.
To the first man in space (and for what it is worth)
I send New Year's Greeting--and come back to earth.
Though I know I can't mention each person by name
To Hyattstown Folk, it is really my aim,
To send New Year's Greeting, most hearty and gay.
To the old, and the young, and all down the Highway.
to the Burdette's Garage--a New Year's Salute,
With the new Pontiacs increasing the loot.
With ice on the roads, and drivers in panic,
They'll be plenty of work for a well-known mechanic.
To the Hyattstown Grocery, Greetings we utter,
It is there all the folks, get their bread and their butter.
And while people shop, and their friends gaily hail,
There are others who sit, and wait for the mail.
To Firemen--Glad Greetings are always in order,

Whether up in Alaska, or South of the Border.
So to Hyattstown Firemen--and their red ambulance
Their carnivals, dinners, and Saturday dance,
May the New Year be one, not of fires, but surprises,
With the Women's Auxiliary, winning all the prizes.
To the Churches--our thanks, and no one will doubt them,
We all will agree we could not do without them.
A Salute to their Ministers--help of their Nation,
And a grateful salute, to each congregation.
Greetings too, to the Old, the infant and minor,
And a Happy New Year, to those at the diner.
A Happy New Year--and we hope many more
To Elizabeth Washburn, and her Brother, next door.
And glad are our hearts, when down in the alley
We see a new colt, with it's good mother, Sally.
To the "Neighborhood Postman", so hearty and hale,
The Jones and Wilsons say "Thanks for our mail".
A bright New Year's Greeting, Mr. Byron, we say,
To the "Man who does Sommerville's work--without pay."
To Ethel Darby and her garden, Happy New Year we hum,
We owe many meals to her famous "green thumb"
She grows lovely flowers--and not just potatoes,
We admire all her flowers--and eat her tomatoes.
Mrs. Cecil, we send you a Greeting sincere,
From us, and all children that you helped to rear.
May the year bring you health, and happiness too,
I'm sure there's no wish that is too good for you.
To the Linthicums all--A Happy New Year,
We appreciate neighbors, and glad you are near.
Happy New Year to the Piglets, and their mothers so fat,
And a Glad Happy New Year, to each kitten and cat.
To Danny and Susan, and year gay and cheery.
And days full of smiles--not one that is teary.
With our wishes so warm, you will never have shivers,
And a Happy New Year--to all of the Rivers.
The old year is waning--The New Year is near--
And no time for greetings to more people dear.
So to all of the world--the great and the small--
I'll say "Happy New Year--Happy New Year to all".

BIBLIOGRAPHY

Ancestral Colonial Families, by Luther W. Welsh p. 72
Baltimore Sun, June 17, 1892 p. 6
Census Records of Montgomery County
Circuit Records of the Montgomery Circuit, M. E. Church
Circuit Records of the Montgomery Circuit, M. P. Church
Diary of Francis Asbury, Lovely Lane, Balto. courtesy, Rev. Schell
Friends of Historic Hyattstown, research on houses and ownership
Frederick County Militia—War of 1812, Mallick and Wright
Frederick-Town Herald June 25, 1803; June 16, 1804; Nov. 24, 1804;
                      Jan 29, 1831 p. 2 col 3
Frederick News-Post, Sept. 3, 1975
Frederick Post 1963
Georgetown Museum, July 10, 1801
History of Hyattstown Christian Church, by Robert L. Price
History of the 12th Massachusetts Volunteers, by Cook 1882
Interviews with Roxye Norwood Anderson
Interviews with Elizabeth Miles Burdette
Interviews with Anice Lee Cecil Dancy
Interview with Ethel Cecil Darby Summer, 1976
Interview with Perry Gray, by Joann Woodson, Feb. 1998
Interview with Sue Houser, October, 1997
Interviews with Frank Linthicum
Interviews with Kitty Linthicum
Interview with Mary Beth Thompson-McDonough October 26, 1997
Interview with Charles Russell Murphy, Mark Walston, October 29, 1979
Interviews with Richie Benson Matthews May 16, 1994 & Jan. 1998
Interview with Ruth Mortimer Price, Mike Dwyer, February 16, 1977
Interview with Louise Thompson October 27, 1997
J. E. B. Stuart, the Last Cavalier, Burke Davis, New York, 1957
J. E. B. Stuart, John W. Thomason, Jr. New York 1930
Lee's Lieutenant's Vol 2., Douglas S. Freeman, New York 1943
Letter of Louis Bissell, August 1, 1864 in possession of Georgette
                      Bissell Allen of Rockville, Md
Life and Campaigns of Major General J. E. B. Stuart, H. B.
                      McClellan   Richmond, 1885
Martinet Map of 1878, Montgomery County, Md
Maryland Journal & True American Nov 29, 1825; Sept. 26, 1826;
                      May 7, 1826; April 9, 1828
Maryland Laws 1805, chapter LXXIX
Maryland Laws 1809, chapter 103 p. 137
Maryland Laws 1812, chapter 49
Maryland Laws 1817, chapter 97

Montgomery County Land Grants

Montgomery County: Schools That Were, by Guy Jewell unpub, 1973

Montgomery County Historical Society

Montgomery County Tax lists

Montgomery Sentinel, 1860; March 1, 1861; July 4, 1872; July 12, 1872; Nov. 12, 1876 Aug. 2, 1878; Nov. 19, 1878; March 4, 1881; Aug 20, 1904; Aug. 26, 1904; Aug 29, 1918

The Retired Officer, Col. John W. Crockett, Aug 1971

United Methodist Historical Society, Balto., Md; Rev. Ed Schell

War Years with J. E. B. Stuart, W. W. Blackford, New York 1945

Washington Star April 26, 1894 p. 1

Williams History and Biographical Record of Western Md.

1850 Manufacturer's Census of Montgomery County, Md.

INDEX